Intellectual Property Rights in the NAM and Other Developing Countries

A Compendium on Laws and Policies

Intellectual Property Rights in the NAM and Other Developing Countries

A Compendium on Laws and Policies

Editor
R. Saha

CENTRE FOR SCIENCE & TECHNOLOGY OF THE NON-ALIGNED AND OTHER DEVELOPING COUNTRIES
(NAM S&T CENTRE)

2006
DAYA PUBLISHING HOUSE
Delhi - 110 035

ISBN 81-7035-439-0

Centre for Science and Technology of the Non-Aligned and Other Developing Countries (NAM S&T Centre)
Core-6A, 2nd Floor, India Habitat Centre, Lodhi Road,
New Delhi-110 003 (India)
Phone: +91-11-24644974, 24645134, Fax: +91-11-24644973
E-mail: namstct@vsnl.com
Website: www.namstct.org

Published by : **Daya Publishing House**
1123/74, Deva Ram Park, Tri Nagar, Delhi - 110 035
Phone: 27383999, Fax: (011) 23244987
e-mail: dayabooks@vsnl.com
website: www.dayabooks.com
Showroom : 4760-61/23, Ansari Road, Darya Ganj
New Delhi - 110 002
Phone: 23245578, 23244987

Laser Typesetting : **Classic Computer Services**
Delhi - 110 035

Printed at : **Chawla Offset Printers**
Delhi - 110 052

Printed in India

FOREWORD

Intellectual Property Rights (IPRs) have been at the centre stage of discussions in developing countries for the last ten years and would continue to occupy an important place in years to come till these countries succeed in evolving a balanced position keeping national and international perspectives, local social, cultural and economic situations in view. Developing countries have many issues in common which cannot be overlooked even in the face of global competition. While accepting the membership of World Trade Organisation (WTO), these countries were not really cognizant of complexities involved in putting together a rearguard action and likely consequences emerging from a new global paradigm. Developing countries have been meeting and consulting with each other on matters related to IPR in many different forums.

The Centre for Science and Technology of the Non-Aligned and other Developing Countries (NAM S&T Centre) has been taking a number of initiatives in bringing together these nations for sharing knowledge in new areas of science and technology through workshops, training programmes and publications. I am very glad that the NAM S&T Centre has decided to bring out a *Compendium on Laws and Policies on Intellectual Property Rights in the NAM and other Developing Countries*, which includes the present IPR laws in 18 countries along with commentaries. I am sure that this publication will be of immense value to all the member countries in understanding the perceptions of various countries and flagging common issues of concern or areas of mutual cooperation for discussions and chalking out an action plan. This would be a step towards helping the members in evolving common positions in international forum.

I would like to place on record my appreciation for all the members and respective authors who have contributed to this Compendium. This publication has been possible with financial and technical support received from the Technology

Information, Forecasting and Assessment Council (TIFAC), Department of Science and Technology, Government of India. I expect that this effort will propel the members in bringing out publications of mutual interest from time to time with full support from the NAM S&T Centre.

V.S. Ramamurthy
Secretary
Ministry of Science & Technology
Department of Science & Technology, Govt. of India
Technology Bhavan, New Mehrauli Road, New Delhi – 110 016

INTRODUCTION

The 21st Century is the era of knowledge and intellect, where a nation's ability to transform knowledge into wealth and social gain through innovations will determine its future. Innovation holds the key to the creation as well as processing of knowledge and thereby to economic development. Consequently, issues of generation, valuation, protection and utilization of intellectual property become critically important all over the world. Intellectual Property (IP), which is the information of commercial importance, derives its intrinsic value from original ideas and is expressed in some discernable ways to be protectable. A functioning IP regime facilitates protection of IP, which encourages transfer of technology in the form of direct foreign investment, joint ventures and licensing.

Intellectual Property Rights (IPR) is the protection of research results in a knowledge-based industry prior to its public distribution. In other words it is a way to safeguard IP. IPR takes a number of forms, such as copyright in case of books, paintings and films, patents for inventions; and trade marks for brand names and product logos. Its underlying objective is to put in place a mechanism that helps the creators to control exploitation of their protected work that ensures appropriate reward for their creative endeavours. Effective and easily enforceable IPR encourages and stimulates the creation of fresh creative works. It also provides a safe and sound system through which protected high quality work of its creator is accessible to general public.

While the basic social objectives of IP protection are as outlined above, it should be noted that the exclusive rights given are generally subject to a number of limitations and exceptions, aimed at fine-tuning the balance between the justifiable interests of holders of the rights and users. The extent of protection and enforcement of these rights vary widely around the world. With IP becoming more important in trade, these differences become a source of tension in international economic relations. The new internationally agreed trade rules for IPR provide a way to introduce more order and predictability and for disputes to be settled more systematically. The WTO's Agreement on TRIPS (Trade-Related Aspects of IPR) that was negotiated in the 1986-94 Uruguay Round, introduced IP rules into the multilateral trading system for the first time. The TRIPS Agreement covers five broad issues including the application of basic principles of the trading system and other international IP agreements, adequate protection to IPR, enforcement of these rights within territories, settlement of disputes on IP between members of the WTO and the transitional arrangements during the period when the new system is being introduced. The Agreement is an attempt to narrow the gaps in the way these rights are protected around the world, and to bring them under common international rules. It establishes minimum levels of protection that each government has to give to the IP of fellow WTO members. In doing so, it strikes a balance between the long-term benefits and possible short-term costs to society. The society benefits in the long term when IP protection encourages creation and invention, especially when the period of protection expires and the creations and inventions enter the public domain. Further, the governments are allowed to reduce any short-term costs through various exceptions, for example, to tackle public health problems, etc.

The obligations under TRIPS apply equally to all member states, with exception to developing countries that enjoy a longer period to implement the applicable changes to their national laws. At the same time it is extremely difficult to generalize the implications of the TRIPS agreement in all developing countries or in a group thereof. Such implications largely vary depending on the differences existing between the IPR laws of a particular country and the standards of the Agreement, the extent of development in different sectors, the per capita income, and the structure of the supply. These countries generally have the established statutory, administrative and judicial framework to safeguard rights, whether they relate to patents, trademarks, copyright or industrial designs, and the protection of IPR continues to be reinforced. Laws setting forth the scope and duration of rights provide the basis for IPR, but these comprise only part of a national system of IPR. Effective protection also depends on the institutions administering the system and the methods used for enforcement.

In order to discuss issues related to IPR causing concern to developing countries including product patents and their implications on national R&D programmes especially in the area of pharmaceuticals, need for granting protection to biological products and micro-organisms and the issues relating to the protection and economics of traditional knowledge, community-based knowledge and bio-diversity, an international conference on "Implications of New IPR Regime under the TRIPS for Developing Countries" was organized in New Delhi during May 19-21, 1999 by the Centre for Science & Technology of the Non-Aligned and Other Developing Countries (NAM S&T Centre) jointly with the Department of Science & Technology (DST), Government of India and the Commonwealth Science Council (CSC). The Conference was attended by 25 participants from 14 countries and was inaugurated by Prof. V.S. Ramamurthy, Secretary DST. Dr. R.A. Mashelkar, Director General, Council of Scientific & Industrial Research (CSIR.), India gave the Keynote Address and Prof. M.Y. Saada, former Vice President, Egyptian Academy of Scientific Research & Technology (ASRT) and the then President of the Governing Council of the NAM S&T Centre, delivered the Presidential address. The other prominent speakers were Prof. J.H. Seyani, Chief Project Officer, CSC, Mr. Shahid Alikhan, former Deputy Director General, World Intellectual Property Organization (WIPO), Dr. M.D. Nair, Former Vice-President of Southern Petrochemical Industries Corporation (SPIC), India, Dr. G. Thyagarajan, Scientific Secretary, Committee on Science and Technology for Developing Countries (COSTED), Chennai, Dr. Y.M. Kohi, Director General, National Commission on Science and Technology (NCST), Tanzania, Eng. Fattouh A. Hamed, President, Patent Office, ASRT Egypt, and Mr. M. Fazlur Rahman, Secretary, Ministry of Science and Technology, Government of Bangladesh. The participants had a group discussion to share their concern on the Article 27(3)(b) of the TRIPS Agreement and the need to revise it and on article 23.4 of TRIPS on geographical indications and the need to extend it to all products and for creating a greater awareness on IPR in developing countries.

This publication brought out by the NAM S&T Centre is largely based on the presentations made at the Conference, that touched upon several aspects of IPR and its protection and issues related to TRIPS as well as the Status Reports submitted by various country participants in this area. The volume also includes articles by the renowned experts on the subject.

On behalf of the Centre, I would like to express our sincere gratitude to the Technology Information, Forecasting and Assessment Council (TIFAC), Department of Science & Technology, Government of India for their generous support towards publication of this book. I would like to put on records the contribution made by Mr. R. Saha, Adviser DST and Director, Patent Facilitation Centre, TIFAC for devoting his precious time for editing this book. I also pay my gratitude to the eminent resource persons and participants of the Conference as well as those who were involved directly or indirectly in making the event a grand success. Last, but not the least, I acknowledge the dynamic involvement of the entire team of the NAM S&T Centre, in particular, Mr. M. Bandyopadhyay, Ms. Garima Sahney and Mr. Pankaj Buttan in compiling the presented papers and giving a shape to the volume.

I hope that the volume would serve as a reference material for the professionals working in the arena of management of IPR and will help the developing countries in working out appropriate strategy, laws, policies and programmes for the protection and exploitation of new technologies and research results for their utilization for the benefit of the society.

Arun P. Kulshreshtha
Director, NAM S&T Centre

CONTENTS

1

TRADE RELATED INTELLECTUAL PROPERTY RIGHTS IN BANGLADESH

Khaliquzzaman

(Chief Scientific Officer, Bangladesh Council of Scientific and Industrial Research, Ramna, Dhaka, Bangladesh)

INTRODUCTION

As a member of WTO and WIPO, Bangladesh is committed to uphold the provisions related to IPR As a member of the group of least developed countries, the provisions of the TRIPS have to implemented in Bangladesh by 2005. Bangladesh has also acceded to Berne convention recently. Rudimentary legal provisions for the protection of Intellectual Property Rights do exist in Bangladesh, in common with the other countries in the sub-continent, in the form of the Patent and design act of 1911 which has been amended from time to time.

Certain provisions of the TRIPS agreement has given rise to wide spread apprehension here in Bangladesh, as elsewhere in the developing countries, especially the article 27 which is up for review in 1999. In the trade regime overseen by the WTO, it is expected that all the countries developed, developing and least developed will be benefited because of the synergistic impact of freer trade and the consequent globalization. It is necessary to ensure that this great hope in the new year does not become an illusion.

The new interdependence generated by the globalization does not necessarily mean symmetrical relationship and equal opportunities for nations at the different levels of scientific and technological development. It is apprehended that implementation of TRIPS provisions will give rise to heavy financial burden for the developing and least developed countries which have very limited scientific and technological capacity. It is necessary to ensure that implementation of TRIPS provisions will not lead to marginalization and a further deterioration in the economic situation of developing countries. In short, it should not be a force for destabilization for the developing countries.

CURRENT STATUS FOR IPR IN BANGLADESH

The existing laws mentioned above with appropriate amendment could take care of the most of the areas covered by the TRIPS agreement which are the following:

1. Copy rights and related rights (*i.e.*, rights of performers, producer of sound recordings and broadcasting organizations)
2. Trademarks including service marks
3. Geographical Indications including appellation of origins
4. Industrial designs
5. Patents including protection of new varieties of plants
6. Layout designs (Topographies) of integrated circuits
7. Protection of undisclosed information including trade secret and test data.

The review and updating of the laws could be completed by 2005 as required in the case of Bangladesh in principle. However, whether such an action will enjoy popular public support is quite another matter. There are vocal intellectual groups and NGOs who have pointed out the apprehensions about the negative impact of the TRIPS provisions. Unless, the public fears are allayed, it will be difficult for any government of place new measures.

ISSUES RELATING TO ARTICLE 27

For ready reference the article is quoted in the following:

Article 27: Patentable Subject Matter

1. Subject to the provisions of paragraphs 2 and 3 patents shall be available for any inventions, whether products or processes, in all fields of technology, provided that they are new, involve an inventive step and are capable of industrial application. Subject to paragraph 4 of Article 65, paragraph 8 of Article 70 and paragraph 3 of this Article, patents shall be available and patent rights enjoyable without discrimination as to the place of invention, the field of technology and whether products are imported or locally produced.
2. Members may exclude from patentability inventions, the prevention within their territory of the commercial exploitation of which is necessary to protect order public of morality, including to protect human, animal or plant life or health or to avoid serious prejudice to the environment, provided that such exclusion is not made merely because the exploitation is prohibited by their law.
3. Members may also exclude from patentability:

   (*a*) diagnostic, therapeutic and surgical methods for the treatment of humans or animals;

(*b*) Plants and animals other than micro-organisms, and essentially biological processes for the production of plants or animals other than non-biological and microbiological processes. However, members shall provide for the protection of plant varieties either by patents or by an effective *sui generic* system or by any combination thereof. The provisions of this subparagraph shall be reviewed four years after the date of entry into force of the WTO Agreement.

Under the article 27 3(b) above, plant varieties are to be protected by patent or an effective *sui generic* system. Under this system, it will be prohibited to use or sell protected variety or any product there off. In such a system farmers will not be able to access freely or reuse seeds. Scientists will be subjected restriction on the use of patented genetic material, which may threaten the survival of public research. This is not a pure commercial problem also. There is also an ethical dimension in it. It must be remembered that current research is only adding to the collective achievement of the mankind as a whole. In last two hundred years, not a single major new grain crop has been added on to what our ancestors had developed. So, today's developments stand on collective human achievements, and the right of the new developments can not be wholly appropriated by any individual or corporation morally.

It is also feared that corporate attempts to get control over agricultural inputs will industrialize the biological world and privatize life form which in turn will promote monoculture, environmentally harmful biotechnology and genetic engineering. The public opinion has already been sensitized on the issue in Bangladesh. The famous Grameen Bank in Bangladesh had to cancel an agreement with Monsanto on genetically engineered variety introduction recently.

The whole issue of plant variety protection was so controversial that the final agreement of the Uruguay round of negotiations require that article 27 3(b) to be reviewed in 1999 whereas the rest of the agreement is to be reviewed in 2000.

OTHER ISSUES AND CONCERNS

The fundamental concern in Bangladesh is that TRIPS related obligation may lead to asymmetrical financial burden on the nation and how to mitigate this negative economic impact. There are estimates of this financial burden on the developing and least developed countries which go as high as 200 billion US $ per year.

It is not the right of an author in the developed world, to earn his living out of his work that concerns us. It is the corporate drive for profit using their scientific and technological capabilities that concerns us. There have been well publicized cases in which companies have marked up the prices of their products in the logarithmicscale compared to cost of production taking advantage of the patent rights. It is thus apprehended that TRIPS related regulations will become the new tools of exploitation of the developing countries. The costs of development of patented products are mostly kept secret and monopoly offered by various regulations can indeed be a tool of exploitation in the wrong hand with the "Gheko" philosophy. May be some where in the agreements, provision of some degree of transparency only the cost of the development of intellectual properties should be included. What we need is the pricing of protected products. Major multinational corporations should also shift substantial part of their R&D bases, commensurate with their market size, to lower cost countries, so that prices of product development can be decreased and some benefit will also accrue to these countries in the process.

CONCLUSION

As a least developed country Bangladesh is faced with multiple problems to provide even the most basic amenities to its population. We are, therefore, not in a position to accept any additional economic and financial liabilities as results of TRIPS. We are not in a position even to estimate with reasonable accuracy what will be our part of the burden. The implementation dead line for the least developed countries should be extended by further 5 years to 2010, so that they can slowly adopt and adapt to the regime without causing too much upheaval in their economy.

Because of the strong public opinion, it may not be practical for us to support any patenting of any type of life form. We, therefore, propose deletion of patenting rights on plant varieties in article 27.3 (b). This article should be reworded to provide a full and unconditional exclusion of all life forms whether they are microorganisms, plants or animals from IPR regime. However, it appears that rights offered under *sui genries* could be used to reduce the negative impact of the article as what constitutes an 'effective' measure has not been defined.

TRIPS reviews in 1999 and 2000 offers us the opportunity to work with other least developed and developing countries to call for changes in the terms of the agreement to reduce the anticipated asymmetrical financial burden on us and we in Bangladesh intend to fully cooperate in such endeavour.

2

STATUS OF INTELLECTUAL PROPERTY IN CAMEROON

Mbah David Akuro

(Geneticist and Development Support, Director of the Department of Valorisation, Ministry of Scientific and Technical Research, B.P., Yaounde)

INTRODUCTION

The question of IPR in traditional African framework in general and Cameroon framework in particular may appear strange at a glance but further examination reveals important foundation on which IPR with more global and modern outlook can be built. In typical Cameroonian society, technologies (*e.g.* iron works-blacksmithing, traditional medicines, etc) and cultural/artistic skills (dances/music, etc) are transferred either within families (usually from parents to offsprings) or across cultures/families (technique or dance) after a ceremony (which may include training the purchaser in the new technique/art or dance). In the first case, the industrial/commercial interest stays within the family while in the second case, it assumes wider dimensions where the seller gets a reward (through the ceremony) for handing over the technology. However, there is no legislative/legal protection of the rights of the owner of the technology.

After independence, realizing the importance of intellectual property rights to development and the need for uniform and efficient protection of intellectual property rights, Cameroon (bilingual in English and French) together with 11 French speaking African countries created the African and Malagasy Industrial Property Office (OAMPI) based on the Libreville Agreement of September 13, 1962. Things have since evolved: Madagascar withdrew while more French speaking African countries joined, membership stands at 15 today OAMPI has become OAPI (African Intellectual Property Organization) (AIOP). (Bangui Agreement, 1977 revised in 1999). The headquarters of the organization is in Yaounde, Cameroon.

CAMEROON WITHIN AIPO (BANGUI AGREEMENT, 1999

As a member of AIPO, Cameroon adheres to the following:

Conventions

1. Paris Convention for the protection of industrial property of march 1883 as revised in Stockholm on July 14, 1967;
2. Berne Convention for the protection of literary and artistic works of September 6, 1886 as revised in Paris on July 14 1971;
3. Universal Convention on authors rights as revised in Paris on July 14 1971;
4. Convention instituting the World Intellectual Property Oranisation of Stockholm, July 14 1967;
5. International Convention for the Protection of Plant Varities of December 2, 1961 as revised in Geneva on December 10, 1972, October 23, 1978 and March 19, 1999;
6. Rome Convention on the Protection of artists/interpreters or executors, producers of phonogrammes and radiodiffusion bodies of 1961.

Treaties

1. Treaty of cooperation in matters of patents of Washington, June 19, 1970
2. Treaty of Nairobi concerning the protection of the Olympic symbol of 1981;
3. Treaty of Budapest on international recognition of depots of micro-organizisms aimed at patenting procedure of 1977;
4. Treaty of Marrakesh creating the World Trade Organization, notably the agreement on aspects of intellectual property rights touching on commerce of April 15, 1994.

Arrangements

1. The Hague Arrangement concerning international depot of drawings or industrial models of November 6, 1925 as revised at the Hague on November 28, 1960;
2. Lisbon Arrangement concerning the protection of appellations of origin and their international registration of October 31, 1958 as revised at Stockholm on July 14, 1967.

Based on this adhesion, Cameroon through the AIPO:

1. Promotes the protection of literary and artistic property as expression of cultural and social values;
2. Stimulates the creation of national authors organization (2);
3. Centralizes, coordinates and diffuses information related to the protection of literary and artistic property.
4. Promotes economic development by efficient protection of intellectual property and related rights; and
5. Trains personnel in intellectual property.

These are stated objectives which AIPO must execute for Cameroon (as well as other member states). Among other obligations to AIPO, Cemeroon pays financial contributions.

SECTORS OF INTEREST (Annexes to the Agreement)

Ten (10) Important sectors are handled:

1. Invention patterns,
2. Utility models,
3. Product/service samples,
4. Industrial drawings and models,
5. Commercial names,
6. Geographic indications,
7. Literary and artistic properties,
8. Protection against unfair competition,
9. Integrated circuits schemes, and
10. Protection of plant varities.

PATENTABLE AND NON-PATENTABLE OBJECTS

To be patented, an invention must:

1. be new involving inventive activities susceptible of industrial application,
2. involve a product, a process or utilization of any of these.

The following are non-patentable:

1. Any invention whose use is contrary to the public order,
2. Invention where only the plant resources, animal breeds, biological processes derived from plants/animals (except micro-organisms and micro biological process and products resulting from these),
3. Surgical methods or therapy as well as diagnostic methods used on humans/animals as well,
4. Computer programmes, etc.

The patent expires after 20 years.

REQUEST FOR PATENTS

Any interested party may address his/her request for patent to:

1. The Ministry of Industrial and Commercial Development (MINDIC) or
2. The AIPO.

The Ministry forwards the request to AIPO. The request, in English or French includes amongst others, the following (all taxes must be paid):

1. Description of invention,

2. Drawings to aid understanding,
3. Explanation indicating extent/scope of the protection
4. Descriptive summary of the description.

For micro-organisms, a receipt by international depot or authority/institution is required.

Since 1964 (*i.e.* 35 years up to 1998), requests for parents by Cameroonians to AIPO (national office of IP protection) have totaled 143 (*i.e.* in average of 4 requests per year). This is 24.4% (25% for Senegal) of all applications by nationals of member states (13 contributor nations). Of the 43 requests made between 1986 and 1992, 15 (*i.e.* 35% had to do with plants largely (medicines, drinks, etc) (4). Public Institutions made only 3/15 requests (Zoology Laboratory of the Faculty of Science, University of Yaounde I, Prof. Jato/IMPM and "Etat Cameroonians"). Other technology generating institutions (*e.g.* Institutes of Agricultural Research did not ask for plant variety protection). Foreigners made more requests for patents than Nationals. Why this state of affairs? Few or no inventions/discoveries? Little or no knowledge of the existence of AIPO or importance of intellectual property protection?

IPR AND LOCAL COMMUNITIES

The closest attempt to address the interest of local communities (*e.g.* farmers) is the stipulation of article 15 of the UPOV convention (2) where on a <<facultative>> basis, farmers may be exempted from the provisions of article 14. So far, plant collections are purchased (if agricultural) at token prices by research/conservation units. The sellers have no benefit from what may result from their sold varieties. Traditional medical practitioners cry foul at medical researchers for << pirating>> their knowledge (*i.e.* plant species with related knowledge on medicinal properties, etc). Token fees (taxes) are also paid to the Ministry of Environment and Forestry (MINEF) for collection of wild plants/animals, MINEF has no concern for what happens or becomes or results from the colle3ctions in relation to industry and commerce. The same situation applies with the Ministry of Scientific and Technical Research (MINREST) which, after issuing a research permit and requiring a copy of the resulting research report, is not concerned with possible, industrial/commercial development/results. This is policy insufficiency requiring improvement. Artists and musicians also talk of piracy and non-payment of royalties. The Ministry of Culture is preparing a law to handle the problem of artist rights (this law may submitted to the parliament in June 1999).

The convention on Biological Diversity (CBD) to which Cameroon is party may provide some improvement(s). The national focal point for the CBD is currently preparing a national biodiversity strategy and action plan as well as a bio-safety law (to regulate development, transfer and use of biotechnology). In the framework of the CBD, an NGO, Bioresources Development and Conservation Programme-Cameroon, together with its bioprospecting partners (Shaman Pharmaceuticals, etc) have had a positive step towards recognition of the benefits/rights of holders of traditional knowledge.

CAMEROON AND TRIPS

Rich in biological diversity (plants, animal, microbiological, ecological), Cameroon is concerned with the provision of GATT/WTO Agreement on Trade Related Aspects of Intellectual Property Rights likely to affect its largely agricultural and rural population in matters of food, security, public health and socio-cultural values. The Ministry of Industrial and Commercial Development (MINDIC) has already organized an "interministerial" meeting to try to examine TRIPS provisions vis-à-vis Cameroon's interest. It is hoped that future meetings on the matter will involve all key stakeholders which, for the public sector, include 7 Ministries (MINEF, MINAGRI, MINEPIA, MINREST, MINREX, MINDIC and MINCUL). It is important to note that Cameroon is a victim of a case of "biopiracy"/"gene piracy" in the 60s through soil sample collections (3) The gene is of great industrial/commercial importance. Hence, micro-organisms cannot be ignored in the matter.

CONCLUSION

African Intellectual Property Organization (AIOP), headquartered in Yaounde, is the national authority for intellectual property protection. AIPO adopts pre-existing conventions (6), treaties (4) and arrangements (2). For its 35 years of existence there have been only 143 patent applications (24% of the total, average of 4 per year) by nationals while non-nationals (*i.e.* from non AIPO member countries) make more applications. For the period 1986-1992, 35% of the applications were related to plant products and or processes. More sensitization of researchers/inventors etc, may be necessary. Current INTELLECTUAL PROPERTY RIGHTS arrangements do not quite protect Cameroon's interest in the areas of biodiversity/biotechnology and traditional knowledge/benefit sharing. Cameroon is yet to take a firm position in these areas and others given the provisions of the TRIPS agreement and the provisions of the convention on biological diversity. Given the dispersion (many ministries that are stakeholders) of efforts, the ministry in charge of INTELLECTUAL PROPERTY RIGHTS protection, MINDIC, must work harder to crystallize a national position/policy in these areas in relation to the TRIPS agreement.

REFERENCES

1. Accord portent revision de l'accord de Bangui du Mars 1977 instutuant une organization AFricaine de la propriete intellectuelle. 24 Fevrier 1999, Bangui
2. Conventin internatinale pour la protection des obtentions vegetales des 2 Decembre 1961, revisec a Geneva le 10 Novembre 1972, le 23 Octobre 1978 et le 19 Mars 1991. UPOV, 1994.
3. Hoechst 1988. In Pflazen Wirksames resistengen gegen phosphinothicia und seial verwendung, European Patent Office: EP275957B1 (C12N 15/31), patent application.
4. Mbantenkhu Mary F and Ndemanou R. 1997. Opportunities and obstacles in the development and trade of living modified organisms resulting from modern bio-technology in Cameroon. IN: Mulongoy K.J. (Ed), Biosafety Needs and Priority Actions for West and Central Africa. PP 19-27. In National Academy of Environment, Geneva, Switzerland.

3

STATUS OF INTELLECTUAL PROPERTY IN CHILE

Eleazar Bravo

(Chief of the Industrial Property Department of Chile received through the Embassy of India in Santiago, Chile)

INTRODUCTION

The Chilean Intellectual Property System accepts the classical division between Industrial Property and Copyright and provides each with different laws. The State intervenes in intellectual property matters through the Industrial Property Department (*www.dpi.cl*) under Ministry of Economy and in Copyright matters through the concerned Department in the Ministry of Education.

INDUSTRIAL PROPERTY

Law No. 19039, which rules industrial Property in Chile, provides that the Industrial Property Department will look after trademarks, invention patents, utility models and industrial designs.

Some requirements have to be complied with in order to qualify for the registration process and some formal procedures also have to be followed; as a general rule, this process may at least imply the possibility that third interested parties may oppose to it and start legal actions; publication in the Official Gazette is also required and applicants may appeal the Resolution of the Industrial Property Department.

The maintenance and custody of Trademark and Invention Patent Registers, dissemination of technological information kept by the Technological Information Office, and Hearing/Resolution of trademark & patent invalidity cases are some of the functions that the Industrial Property Department has been entrusted with.

COPYRIGHT

Law 17336 rules copyright. The concerned Department, which is under the Ministry of Education, is in charge of the maintenance and custody of a Copyright Register. The procedure is structured on the basis of a simple deposit and there is no possibility of contravention by third parties during the registration process.

The address of the Copyright Department is 247 San Isidro, Santiago; Phone (56-2) 2222663, Santiago – Chile.

The Copyright Department also looks after the registration of software. Software is therefore only protected by copyright laws.

REGISTRATION OF INDUSTRIAL PROPERTY RIGHTS

It is the role of the Industrial Property Department to register trademarks or patents. The Address of the Industrial Property Department is 920 Moneda, Piso 10, Santiago Centro, Chile; Phone: (56-2) 6883124 – 6986413. The Industrial Property Department keeps a comprehensive data base which is freely open to the public and which allows them to search for information, get information on the registration procedure, obtain copies of the concerned laws, obtain copies of various forms, search the state of techniques and have access to the complete data base of the Department. They can also get information on the current status of their applications, as all the information available with the Department is published in their website (www.proind.gov.cl) with only a few hours difference.

INTERNATIONAL LAWS

Chile is a signatory country of a series of international treaties and agreements on industrial property:

1. Convention establishing the World Intellectual Property Organisation (WIPO Convention, 1976)
2. Paris Convention ((Paris Union, 1991)
3. Berne Convention for the protection of literary and artisdic works (Berne Union, 1970)
4. Convention for the protection of Phonogram producers (Rome Convention, 1974)
5. Convention for the protection of phonograms, against non-authorized duplication of such phonograms. (Phonograms Convention, 1977)
6. Treaty for the protection of the Olympics Symbol (Nairobi Treaty, 1981)
7. Treaty for the registration of audio-visual works (FRT Union, 1993)
8. Convention for the protection of new vegetable varieties (1996)
9. Agreement on Trade Related Intellectual Property Aspects (TRIPS)
10. The 1996 WIPO Treaty on Copyright and Interpretation/Execution of Phonograms.

Civil Questions

Disputes related to compensations for damages and compensations of civil origin related to industrial property fall under the jurisdiction of the Ordinary Courts of Justice. Intellectual Property Laws in Chile do not include any special regulation in this respect.

Criminal Issues

Faults and crimes related to intellectual property are identified in the concerned intellectual property law. However, it is for the Ordinary Courts of Justice to try such cases and apply sanctions. It is a crime to produce or sell false merchandise, and the sanction imposed on those who infringe the law is a penalty ranging from UTM 100 to UTM 500. (UTM 1 = US$ 50 approx.) The possibility that false merchandise may be confiscated is also contemplated in the law.

Reforms Under Discussion

Chile, in its condition as a member state of the WTO and its allied instruments, is amending its laws to international standards. Chile is, therefore, working on the harmonization of its laws by establishing protections to Integrated Circuits Schemes; creating a national register of Geographical Indications and Denominations of Origin under the control and supervision of the future Institute of Intellectual Property; establishing rules and regulations in respect of non disseminated information and imposing civil and criminal sanctions against non-authorized dissemination of information; incorporating industrial drawings as a new category of copyright; protecting Data Bases; incorporating clauses on the lease of copyright; taking steps to confiscate false merchandise at the borders with the help of the National Custom Service; elaborating an Infraction Control System with expeditious devices for the calculation of compensations; establishing new criminal figures for the control and repression of illegal copying.

The National Congress is currently holding discussions on three Intellectual Property Reform Bills, which are intended to amend the existing law.

LAW ON INDUSTRIAL PROPERTY (*)

Law N 19.039 (**)

(*) Unofficial translation prepared by the Chilean Association on Industrial Property (ACHIPI)

(**) Published in the Official Gazette on 25th January 1991 and is in force as from September 30, 1991.

Title I: COMMON PROVISIONS

Article 1

This law contains the provisions applicable to industrial privileges and the protection of industrial property rights. The referred privileges include trademarks, patents of invention, utility models, industrial designs and other protection titles that the law may establish.

Article 2

Any natural or legal person, either national or foreign, may enjoy the industrial property rights warranted by the Constitution, by previously procuring the corresponding protection title pursuant to the provisions of this law. The natural or legal persons living abroad shall, to the effects of this law, appoint an agent or representative in Chile.

Article 3

The proceeding of the applications, the granting of titles and other services related to industrial property are the competence of the Department of Industrial Property, hereinafter the "Department" dependent from the Ministry of Economy, Reconstruction and Development.

Applications may be filed personally or by proxy.

Article 4

Upon acceptance of an application for proceeding, an abstract of the same shall be published in the Official Gazette in the manner established by the Regulations.

Article 5

Any interested party may oppose the application filed with the Department within a period of 30 days from the date of publication of the abstract.

The term set forth in the previous paragraph shall be of 60 days in the case of an application for a patent of invention.

Article 6

Upon expiration of the above mentioned term, the Head of the Department shall order an expert report in respect of applications for patents of invention, utility models and industrial designs with the purpose of ascertaining if the requirements established in articles 32, 56 and 62 of this law are met.

Article 7

In procedures relating to patents of invention, utility models and industrial designs applicants shall be granted a period of 60 days in order to state their rights. In the case of trademarks, such term will be of 30 days.

Article 8

If there are substantial and relevant controversial facts, the case will be received for a term of 60 days, this period being extendible for up to another 60 days if any of the parties has his domicile abroad. In the case of trademark cases, the time allowed for producing evidence will be 30 days, extendible for another 30 days in cases duly qualified by the Head of the Department.

Article 9

Once the decision to make an expert report is issued, the latter shall be made within the term of 120 days from acceptance of the charge by the expert. This period may be extended up to another 120 days in cases where, in the opinion of the Head of the Department, it is so required.

The expert´s report shall be made known to the interested parties who will have 120 days from notification to present the remarks they deem convenient. This term may be extended only once, upon request of an interested party up to 120 days.

Article 10

The cost of the expert work shall include, the fees of the expert and the necessary expenses for his perfomance, which shall be charged to the applicant of the patent of invention, utility model or industrial design or to the plaintiff seeking the invalidation of these privileges.

Article 11

The terms of days established in this law is unpostponable only working days are counted. To this effect Saturday shall be considered as a non working day.

Article 12

In these procedures the parties may make use of all the customary means of proof in this type of matters and of those set forth in the Code of Civil Procedure, excluding oral evidence.

In addition, in these procedures, the provisions of paragraph two of article 64 of the mentioned Code shall apply.

Article 13

Notices shall be given according to the rules set forth in the Regulations.

Article 14

Industrial property rights are transmissible in case of death and may be the object of any kind of juridical act, which shall be executed by public deed and annotated on the margin of the respective registration.

Notwithstanding, in the case of transfer of applications for the registration of industrial privileges, a private instrument executed before a notary public will suffice and subsequent annotation will not be necessary. In any event, the Trademark registrations are indivisible and none of the elements or characteristics covered by the title may be transferred partially and separately.

Article 15

Powers of attorney related to industrial property may be granted by public deed or by private instrument signed before a notary public or before an authorized Civil Register Official in those municipalities where there is not a notary. Powers of attorney coming from abroad may be executed or legalized before the respective Chilean Consul with no other subsequent formality; or in the manner established in article 345 of the Code of Civil Procedure.

Article 16

Offenses established hereunder are of criminal action and will be tried in accordance with the provisions of ordinary trials on crimes or simple offenses.

In these trials evidence will be appreciated in equity and the Department must be heard before sentence is pronounced.

Article 17

Opposition trials, those related to invalidation of registrations or of assignments, as well as any claim regarding the validity or effects thereof, or regarding industrial property rights in general, shall be tried before the Head of the Department of Industrial Property, in accordance with the formalities established hereunder and to those provided by the Regulations.

The judgment pronounced shall be justified and in its form shall comply, to the extent possible, with the provisions of article 170 of the Code of Civil Procedure.

Resolutions containing or grounded on manifest factual errors may be corrected ex -officio or upon request of the parties within five days from the date of notice.

Final decisions of the Head of the Department shall be subject to be filed within the term of 15 days from the notice of the decision, to be heard by the court of arbitration to which the following clauses refer.

The Industrial Property Court of Arbitration will be composed of three members who will be appointed, every two years, by the Minister of Economy, Reconstruction and Development, one of which will be of the latter's own election, another will be proposed by the President of the State Defense Council from among his body of attorneys and the third one to be elected from a list of three names to be presented by the Court of Appeals of Santiago. The Court shall also have a Secretary-Lawyer who will be an officer of the Ministry of Economy, Reconstruction and Development.

For the preparation of the list of three names mentioned above, the Court of Appeals of Santiago will include therein persons having performed as judges of any Court of Appeals in the country or as associate judges integrating same.

When the Court of Arbitration is to hear cases that require a specialized knowledge, it may appoint a technical expert, the cost of which shall be paid by the apellant.

The Court of Arbitration shall meet as many times as necessary and decided by the Court itself. Its members will be paid by the budget of the Ministry of Economy, Reconstruction and Development, for their attendance to each session in the manner prescribed by the regulations. Such payment shall be compatible with any other of Government origin. Regulations shall establish the working modalities of the Court and administrative support.

Article 18

The granting of patents of invention, utility models and industrial designs shall be subject to payment of a fee equal to one monthly "unidad tributaria" (1)for every five years in which the privilege is granted.

Precautionary patents shall be subject to payment of a fee equal to one half "unidad tributaria".

Registration of trademarks shall be subject to payment of a fee equal to two "unidades tributarias". One half unidad tributaria shall be paid upon filing the application, without which no legal proceeding shall not start. Upon acceptance of the application, payment of the fee will be completed and, if rejected, the amount paid will remain for fiscal benefit.

Renewal of trademark registrations shall be subject to payment of twice the fee prescribed in the above paragraph.

The filing of appeals in cases related to trademarks, patents of invention, utility models and industrial designs, will be subject to payment of a fee equal to two "unidades tributarias". In case of acceptance of the appeal, the Court of Arbitration will order the refund of the amount paid in accordance with the procedure set forth by the regulations.

Recording of ownership transfers, licenses of use, pledges and change of names and any other kind of encumbrances that may affect a patent of invention, utility model, industrial design or trademark, will be made by previous payment of a fee equal to one half "unidad tributaria". The aforementioned acts pointed out shall not be applicable to third parties if not recorded with the Department.

All fees established in this article shall be for Fiscal benefit, and payment thereof shall be accredited with the Department of Industrial Property within the term of 60 days from the date of the decision that authorizes recording in the respective registry, without which the application will be considered abandoned, and shall be placed in the archives.

Registrations of trademarks which distinguish services and are limited to one or more provinces will be understood as being extensive to all the national territory.

Registrations of trademarks made by provinces to protect commercial establishments will be understood to cover all the region or regions where the respective provinces are a part of.

The holders of the registrations referred to in the two preceding paragraphs which, by virtue of this article, expand the territorial protection scope of their trademarks, shall not offer services or install commercial establishments covered by such trademarks in the same provinces for which same or similar trademarks are registered regarding services or establishments of same line of business, under warning of incurring in the infringement contemplated in letter a) of article 28 of this law.

Note of Translator: "Unidad Tributaria" is an official economic index existing in Chile which value is subject to adjustment on a monthly basis according to several economic indexes.

Title II: TRADEMARKS

Article 19

A trademark is any visible, innovating and characteristic sign to distinguish products, services or industrial or commercial establishments.

The propaganda or advertising phrases may also be registered, provided they tied to or associated to a registered trademark of the product, service or commercial or industrial establishment for use therein. The propaganda phrase shall necessarily contain the trademark object of the advertising.

If a trademark is applied for that contains words, prefixes, suffixes or common use roots which are of a generic nature, indicative or descriptive, the privilege may be granted, duly putting on record that it is granted without protection to the referred elements individually considered. Likewise, the trademark registration consisting in a label, protects if as a whole and not each the elements that conform it.

If applicant gives a name to the label, the word that constitutes this name shall be the one to appear outstanding and shall also enjoy trademark protection, but not the rest of the words that may be contained in the label, record of which shall be left in the registry.

Article 20

The following cannot be registered as a trademark:

(*a*) Coat of arms, flags or any other symbols, the names or initials of any State, of international organizations and of State public services.

(*b*) Technical or scientific denominations in respect of the object to which they are destined, common international denominations recommended by the World Health Organization and those indicative of therapeutic action.

(*c*) The name, pen name or picture of any natural person, except if consent is given by him or his heirs, if deceased. However, names of historical celebrities may be registered provided at least 50 years from his/her death have elapsed and provided it does not affect his/her honor. However, names of persons cannot be registered when this constitutes an infringement of paragraphs (*e*), (*f*), (*g*) and (*h*).

(*d*) Those that reproduce or imitate signs or official guarantee control punches adopted by a State, without its authorization; and those that reproduce or imitate medals, diplomas or honors granted in national or foreign exhibitions the registration of which is requested by a person other than the one who obtained it.

(*e*) The expressions used to indicate the kind, nature, origin, nationality, source, destination, weight, value or quality of the products, services or establishments; those of general use in trade to name a certain kind of products, services or establishments, and those that do not exhibit an innovating feature or describe the products, services or establishments to which they must be applied.

(*f*) Those that may induce to error or deceit regarding source, quality or kind of the products, services or establishments.

(*g*) Trademarks that are the same or those which graphically or phonetically resemble in a manner likely to produce confusion with others registered abroad for the same products, services or commercial and/or industrial establishments provided they enjoy fame and notoriety.

If registration is rejected or invalidated for this reason, the foreign owner shall within 90 days apply for registration of the trademark; failure to do so, the trademark may be requested by any person, priority being given to the one whose application for registration was rejected or was the subject of the invalidation.

(*h*) Those that are identical or which graphically or phonetically resemble, in a confusingly manner, others already registered or validly applied for earlier in the same class.

(*i*) The shape, color, decorations and accessories either of products or of containers.

(*j*) Those contrary to public order, morality and good behavior, comprising therein the principles of fair competition and business ethics.

Article 21

Registration of trademarks shall be made with the Department and recording applications will be filed in compliance with the prescriptions and in the manner set forth in the Regulations.

Article 22

Before the Registrar of Trademarks may accept a trademark application, the Department shall make a search or preventive examination to establish if one of the reasons for non-registration set forth in article 20 applies.

The decision of the registrar of Trademarks denying proceedings for an application pursuant to article 4 of this law may be the subject of a complaint to the Head of the Department within 20 days.

Article 23

Each trademark may be applied for and registered for only certain products, or for one or more classes of the International Classification. In the same manner, services may only be applied for and recorded when they are specific and determined from the different classes of the International Classification. Likewise, trademarks may be applied for and registered to distinguish industrial or commercial manufacturing or marketing establishments in association with one or several classes of certain products; and propaganda phrases for application in the advertising of trademarks already registered.

To the effects of payment of fees, the application or recording of a trademark in each class will be considered as a different application or registration.

Trademark registrations that distinguish the products, services and industrial establishments shall be valid for all the territory of the Republic.

Trademark registrations protecting commercial establishments are valid only for the region in which the establishment is located. If the interested party wishes to make extensive to other regions the property of the same trademark, he shall state so in his application for registration, and shall pay the fee corresponding to a registration by each region.

Article 24

The registration of a trademark shall have duration of ten years, from the date of registration in the corresponding registry. Holder will have a right to request renewal for equal periods during its life or in the 30 days following expiration of such period.

Article 25

Any brand recorded and used in commerce shall visibly exhibit the words "Marca Registrada" or the initials "M:R:" or letter "R" inside a circle. Omission of this requirement does not affect the validity of the trademark, but those who fail to comply with this provision cannot make use of the penal actions referred to in this law.

Article 26

Invalidation of a trademark registration may be requested when any of the prohibitions established in article 20 of this act is infringed.

Article 27

The action of invalidation of the registration of a trademark cannot be started after 5 years from the date of registration. Once such period has elapsed the Head of the Department will officially declare it, not accepting proceedings for invalidation.

Article 28

The following will be condemned to pay a fine in favor of the government of 100 to 500 "unidades tributarias":

(*a*) Those who use maliciously a trademark that is the same or similar to the one already registered in the same class of the classification in force.

(*b*) Those who defraud making use of a trademark.

(*c*) Those perpetrating fraud by using or imitating through advertising a trademark in the same class of the Classification.

(*d*) Those who use a non-registered expired or invalidated trademark, with the indications corresponding to a trademark.

(*e*) Those that make use of containers or packing bearing a trademark that is not their property, without it being previously erased, except in the case that the marked packing is destined to pack products of a class other than the one protected by the trademark.

He who relapses within the last five years into one of the offenses contemplated in this article, will be applied a fine that may be up to twice the previous one.

Article 29

Those condemned according to the preceding article shall be obliged to pay costs and damages to the owner of the trademark.

The implements and elements used in the forgery or imitation and the objects with a forged trademark shall be seized to the benefit of the owner of the trademark. The Judge for the case may immediately order its attachment, without prejudice of his authority to take the appropriate preventive measures.

Article 30

Where a non registered trademark is being used by one or more persons at a time, the person that registers same cannot persecute the responsibility of those who continue to use it until, al least, 120 days have elapsed from the date of registration.

Title III: PATENTS OF INVENTION

Article 31

Invention is any solution of a technical problem that originates an industrial activity. An invention may consist of a product or a process or be related thereto.

Patent is the exclusive right granted by the State to protect an invention. This law determines the effects, obligations and limitations inherent to the patent.

Article 32

An invention is patentable if it is new, involves an inventive step and is industrially applicable.

Article 33

An invention is new when if it is not anticipated by prior art. Prior art shall consist of everything disclosed to the public, anywhere in the world, by publication in tangible form or, by the sale or marketing, the use or any other means, before the date of filing the patent application in Chile. Additionally, prior art shall comprise the contents of a patent application in process before the Department and whose filing date is prior to that of the application being examined.

Article 34

In case a patent has been previously applied for abroad, the interested party will have priority for the term of one year, from the date of it's filing in the country of origin, to file the application in Chile.

Article 35

An invention shall be considered as involving an inventive step if, for a person having ordinary skill in the relevant technical matter, it does not appear obvious or as an evident result from the state of art.

Article 36

An invention shall be considered industrially applicable when its object can, in principle, be produced or used in any type of industry. To this effect, the expression "industry" shall be construed in its broadest sense, including activities such as: manufacture, mining, construction, craftmanship, agriculture, forestry and fishing.

Article 37

The following are not considered inventions and remain excluded from the patent protection under this law:

(*a*) Discoveries, scientific theories and mathematical methods.

(*b*) The plant varieties and animal breeds.

(*c*) The systems, methods, principles or economic, and financial, commercial plans of simple ascertainment and supervision, and those referred to purely mental or intelectual activities or to gambling matters.

(*d*) The methods for surgical or therapeutic treatment of the human or animal body, as well as the diagnosis methods applied to the human or animal body, except those products destined to put into practice one of these methods.

(*e*) The new use of articles, objects or elements known and used for certain purposes and the change in shape, dimensions, proportions and materials of the object requested unless they result in essential modifications of its qualities or, with its use derive in the solving of a technical problem which did not have a solution before.

Article 38

Inventions contrary to the law, public order and security of the State; or to morality and good habits, as well as those presented by who is not its legitimate owner, shall not be patentable.

Article 39

Patents of invention shall be granted for a non-renewable term of 15 years.

Notwithstanding the provisions of article 34, patents applied for in Chile for inventions already patented or whose application is pending abroad, shall be granted only for the time that is still left for the right to expire in the country in where patent was applied for or obtained, without exceeding the term set forth in the above paragraph.

Article 40

Improvements shall be considered to be the modifications introduced to an already known invention, provided it is innovating and has notorious and relevant advantages in relation to the original invention.

Article 41

The application for patents related to inventions already patented in the country and provided these are in force, shall be filed by their authors and will be subject to the following provisions:

(*a*) If the person who made the improvement is the owner of the original invention, he will be granted the patent for the time that is left to complete the term of the original patent.

(*b*) If the person who made the improvement is a third party and the term of the granting of the patent on which the improvements have a bearing is still in force, the patent may be granted only if the original inventor authorizes the second inventor to use the original idea jointly with the innovations in question. The patent may be granted to both inventors jointly or only. The patent may be granted to both inventors jointly or only to one of them, the agreement of which shall be recorded in a document attached to the respective file.

(*c*) In the absence of an agreement, the author of the improvement may request a patent on it. When this circumstance occurs, the date of start of the protection and the term of grant of the complementary patent will be decided by the Head of the Department. The inventor shall advise the Department of his intention in a period of 90 day from the date of the original application.

Article 42

Any inventor resident in the country who is studying an invention and needs to practice experiences or have constructed any device that forces him to disclose his idea, may provisionally protect his rights against possible usurpations by requesting, to that effect, a certificate of protection or precautionary patent that the Department will grant him for one year prior payment of the respective fee.

This certificate shall give its owner preferential legal right over any other person who during the year of protection seeks to request privileges on the same matter. In any case the duration of the final patent will be counted from the application for precautionary patent.

If the owner of a precautionary patent does not apply for the final patent in one year, the invention will become of public domain.

Article 43

Upon filing the application with the Department, a preliminary examination shall be made to ascertain that at least the following data are accompanied:

(*a*) A Summary of the invention

(*b*) A description of the invention

(*c*) Document containing claims

(*d*) Drawings of the invention, when appropriate.

The description shall be clear and complete in such a manner as to allow an expert in the matter to carry out the invention without the need of further data.

When from the examination of the claims of patent applied for it may be inferred that it corresponds to a utility model or to an industrial design, it will be examined and treated as such, keeping the priority acquired.

Article 44

The statements of novelty, ownership and usefulness of the invention are to be made by the applicant who will issue them under his responsibility.

The granting of a patent does not mean that the State warrants the need and accurateness of the statements made by the applicant in the application and in the description.

Article 45

If the data accompanied are not complete, absence thereof may be obviated within 40 days following notification of the remarks. In this case, the valid date will be that of the initial application. Otherwise it will be considered as not filed and the date of the application will be that of the correction or new filing.

Applications that do not meet any other requirement for proceeding within the terms set forth in this law or in the Regulations, shall be considered abandoned and shall be placed in the archives. In this case, the applicant may ask for having his application reinstated within 120 days from the date of abandonment, without losing the date of priority of the application.

Article 46

Applicants of patents already applied for abroad shall furnish the results of the search and the examination made by the foreign office, in case they were issued, whether or not a patent was finally granted.

Article 47

All data concerning the patent applied for shall be kept in the Department and available to the public after the publication referred to in article 4.

Article 48

Upon approval of the grant and after accrediting payment of the corresponding fees, the interested party will be granted the patent and a certificate will be issued granting protection as of the date on which the application was filed.

Article 49

The owner of a patent shall enjoy the exclusive right to produce, sell or market in any way the product or object of the invention and, in general, to exploit it in any other way.

This privilege is extensive to all the territory of the Republic until expiration of the term for which the patent was granted.

Article 50

A patent may be invalidated in any of the following circumstances:

(*a*) When the person who has obtained the patent license is not the inventor or his assignee.

(*b*) When the grant of the patent was based on expert reports that are wrong or obviously deficient.

(*c*) When the privilege is granted in violation of the provisions on patentability and requirements thereof, in accordance with the provisions of this law.

The invalidation action of a patent of invention may be excercised at any time during a term of 10 years.

Article 51

Non voluntary licenses will only be granted in the case the patentee incurs in monopolistic abuse according to the Resolutory Commission of Decree-law No.211 of 1973, which will be the Agency in charge of determining the existence of the situation denounced and deciding accordingly.

The decision of the Commission shall be qualify, at least, the following aspects:

(*a*) The existence of a situation of monopolistic abuse.

(*b*) In the case where such pronouncement is positive, the verdict of the Commission shall establish the conditions in which licensee shall work the license, the term for which the license is granted and the amount of compensation that will be paid periodically by whoever uses the non voluntary license to the owner of the patent.

(*c*) In order to analyze the financial and accounting statements the standards applicable by the Superintendence of Securities and Insurance to open stock companies shall apply.

Article 52

Fines of 100 to 500 "unidades tributarias" for fiscal benefit, shall be the penalty to those:

(*a*) Who defraud another using a non-patented object, with indications corresponding to a patent, or any other similar deceit?

(*b*) Who without due authorization manufacture, market or import with selling purposes a patented invention?

(*c*) Who defraud making use of a patented process? This regulation will not apply in case the use of patented process is made for purely experimental or teaching purposes.

(*d*) Who commit fraud by imitating a patented invention?

(*e*) Who maliciously imitate or use an invention with a pending patent applications, provided a patent is finally granted?

The persons condemned shall be obliged to pay costs and damages to the owner of the patent.

The implements and elements used in the perpetration of any of the crimes mentioned in this article and the objects produced illegally will be confiscated for the benefit of the owner of the patent. Likewise, the judge of the case may immediately order its seizure without prejudice to adopting the appropriate preventive measures.

Recurrence will be punished with twice the fines set forth in paragraph one.

Article 53

Any patented object shall bear the indication of the number of the patent whether in the product itself or in the container and the expression "Patent of Invention" shall be placed visibly, or the initials "P:I:" and number of the privilege.

The only exception to this obligation is the procedures where, by their very nature, it is not possible to apply this requirement.

Omission to this requirement does not affect the validity of the patent, but those who fail to meet this provision will not be able to exercise the penal actions provided for in this law.

In the case of pending applications this situation should be mentioned, whenever the products related to the application are manufactured, marketed or imported with commercial purposes.

Title IV: UTILITY MODELS

Article 54

Utility models shall be understood as the instruments, devices, tools, mechanisms and objects or parts thereof, where the form may be claimed, both in its external aspect and in its functioning and provided such form results in some usefulness, that is, that may contribute to their function with benefit, advantage or technical effect that they lacked before.

Article 55

The provisions of Title III, related to patents of invention, are applicable, where appropriate, to utility models, without prejudice of the special provisions contained in this title.

Article 56

A utility model shall be patentable if it is new and industrially applicable.

A privilege will not be granted when the utility model only presents minor or secondary differences that contribute no discernible utility characteristic regarding previous inventions or utility models.

Application for a utility model may only refer to an industrial object, without prejudice that several elements or aspects of such object may be claimed in the same application.

Article 57

Utility model protection shall be granted for non renewable period of 10 years, from the date of application.

Article 58

Upon filing the application with the Department, a preliminary examination will be made to ascertain that at least the following documents are accompanied:

(*a*) A summary of the utility model.

(*b*) A description of the utility model.

(*c*) Document containing claims.

(*d*) Drawings of utility models.

Article 59

Any utility model shall bear in a visible manner the expression "Utility Model" or the initials and numbers of the privilege. Omission of this requirement does not affect validity of the utility model but deprives the owner from the possibility of using the penal actions established in this law.

Article 60

An invalidation of the utility model is possible for the same reasons set forth in article 50.

Article 61

Fines of 100 to 500 "unidades tributarias" for fiscal benefit, shall be the penalty to those:

(*a*) Who defraud another making use of a non patented object, with indications corresponding to utility model license or using another similar deceit.

(*b*) Who without due authorization manufacture, market or import with selling purposes, a utility model.

(*c*) Who commit fraud by imitating a utility model.

(*d*) Who maliciously imitate or use a utility model with pending application, provided the title is finally granted.

The persons condemned will be obliged to pay costs and damages to owner of the utility model.

The devices and elements used in the perpetration of any of the crimes mentioned in this article and the objects produced illegally will be confiscated in favor of owner of the utility model. Likewise, the judge of the case may immediately order their seizure without prejudice to adopting appropriate preventive measures.

Recurrence will be punished with twice the fine set forth in paragraph one.

Title V: INDUSTRIAL DESIGNS

Article 62

Industrial design shall comprise any tridimensional form associated or not with colors, and any industrial or craftsmanship goods serving as pattern for the manufacture of other units which is distinguished from its similar, by its form, geometrical configuration, ornamentation or combination thereof, provided such features give it a special aspect perceptible to sight, in such a way as to give it an original, new and different physiognomy.

Containers are comprised among the articles that may be protected as industrial designs, provided they meet the conditions of novelty and originality mentioned before.

Clothing of any nature may not be protected as industrial designs.

Article 63

The provisions in Title III relating to patents of invention are applicable, where appropriate, to industrial designs, without prejudice of the special provisions contained in this article.

The invalidation of industrial designs is possible for the same reasons set forth in article 50.

Article 64

Any application for industrial design privilege shall be made by filing at least the following documents:

(*a*) Application
(*b*) Description
(*c*) Drawing
(*d*) Prototype or model, where appropriate.

Article 65

Industrial designs shall be granted for non-renewable period of 10 years from the date of application.

Article 66

Any industrial design shall visibly exhibit the expression "Industrial Design" or the initials and number of the privilege. Omission of this requirement does not affect the validity of the industrial design, but deprives its holder from the possibility of using the penal actions established in the following article.

Article 67

Fines for fiscal benefit of 100 to 500 "unidades tributarias" shall be the penalty to those:

(*a*) Who without duly authorization manufacture, market or import with commercial purposes, a registered industrial design.
(*b*) Who maliciously imitate a registered industrial design.
(*c*) Who maliciously imitate or make use of an industrial design the application of which is pending, provided the privilege is finally granted

The person condemned will be obliged to pay costs and damages to owner of the privilege.

The implements and elements used in the perpetration of any of the crimes mentioned in this article and objects produced illegally will be seized in favor of owner of the privilege. Likewise, the judge of the case may immediately order their seizure, without prejudice to adopting the appropriate preventive measures.

The recurrence will be punished with twice the fine set forth in clause one.

Title VI: SERVICE INVENTIONS

Article 68

In work and service contracts, the nature of which is the fulfillment of an inventive or creative activity, the authority to request the privilege as well as the eventual industrial property rights, will belong solely to whoever ordered the service, unless express stipulation to the contrary.

Article 69

The authority to request the privilege, as well as the eventual industrial property rights arising from inventions made by the worker who, according to his work contract, is not obliged to perform an inventive or creative function, will belong exclusively to him.

However, if to carry out the invention he has evidently benefited from knowledge acquired within the enterprise and uses means furnished by it, such authority and right will belong to employer, in which case the latter must grant worker an additional compensation to be agreed between the parties.

The above shall be applicable to the person who obtains an invention in excess of the framework of the one that was ordered.

Article 70

The power to request the respective privilege as well as the eventual industrial property rights arising from the inventive and creative activities of individuals hired in a dependent or independent relationship, by universities or research institutions included in Decree Law No. 1.263 of 1975, shall belong to the latter or to whom they determine, without prejudice to the bylaws of such agencies which may regulate the patterns in which inventor or creator participates in the benefits obtained for his work.

Article 71

The rights established on behalf of worker in the preceding articles, may not be waived before the granting of the patent or the utility mode. Any clause to the contrary shall be considered as not written.

All the disputes concerning the implementation of this title shall be the competence of the Court of Arbitration referred to in paragraphs five to eight of article 17 of this law.

Title VII: DEROGATORY PROVISIONS

Article 72

Decree-law No. 958 of 1931 on Industrial Property, articles 16 and 17 of law No. 18.591; article 38 of law No. 18.681; and law No. 18.935 are revoked.

Title VIII: TRANSITIONAL PROVISIONS

Article 1

Notwithstanding the provisions of paragraph second of article 39 of this law, above patents may be applied for medicines of any kind, medicine and drug preparations and preparations and chemical reactions thereof, provided applications are filed in their country of origin only after the date of this law has entered into forced.

Article 2

Article 72 shall apply to terms that are initiated and decisions notified in advance of the entering into force of this law.

Appeals pending with the Arbitration Commission referred to in article 17 of Decree-Law No. 958 of 1931, shall be transferred to the Court of Arbitration created by article 17 of this law. These appeals will be exempt from paying the fee referred to in article 18.

Article 3

The applications for patents of invention and industrial models that are pending and do not infringe this law, shall continue their proceedings in accordance to the provisions of Decree-Law No. 958 of 1931.

However, within the 120 days following the entering into force of this law, applicants that deem it convenient may file a new application which will adjust to the provisions of this law and shall maintain the priority of the original application.

Article 4

This law will enter into force on the day of publication in the Official Gazette of the Regulations that the President of the Republic shall issue in its regard, which will be prepared within the term of 1 year from the publication of this law.

4

Intellectual Property Rights and the Expected Changes in the Light of the General Agreement on Tariffs and Trade (GATT) and Status Report for the Egyptian Patent Office

Fattouh Abdel Gelil Hamed

(President, Egyptian Patent Office, Cairo, Egypt)

HISTORICAL BACKGROUND ON THE ESTABLISHMENT AND DEVELOPMENT OF GATT

The Second World War was ended in 1945. It accounted for the destruction and devastation of the economies of the majority of countries all over the world.

Intensified efforts had started to formulate a new world characterized by its vital and accurately performed global economy.

International Monetary Fund (IMF) was established in 1947 in the aim supervising the world's monetary system and working towards its liberalization through:

- Excchange rate,
- Interest rate,
- Banks' credit ceilings,

- Balances of payments and other aspects relate with the world's monetary system.

The International Bank for Reconstruction and Development (IBRD) was established in 1947, in the aim of supervising the International financial system and working towards its liberalization through long term loans for developmental processes, best utilization of economic resources and encouraging private investment.

A general agreement for international trade, The General Agreement on Tariffs and Trade (GATT) was signed in 1947 by 23 countries, all of which developed countries.

This agreement came into force in 1948, and its main objective was to work towards the liberalization of international trade.

Since its inception, The GATT had held 8 rounds for negotiations:

- The first round was held in 1957, at Geneva
- The last round was held in 1986 at Uruguay.

Through the period between the first and the last rounds, a large number of countries acceded to the Agreement – 117 countries.

The last Uruguay Round ended up with the establishment of a new organization, World Trade Organization (WTO), in the aim of supervising the international trade and working towards its liberalization.

The representatives of the member states (117 countries) initialed in 1993 the establishment of this organization.

The Ministers of Foreign Trade of member states signed in 16 April 1994 at Marrakech (Morocco) as a preliminary stage before submitting the agreement to the Parliaments of the member states for ratification.

The agreement entered into force in the first of January 1995.

THE PRINCIPLES OF THE GATT AGREEMENT, FIVE

Principle of the Most Favoured Nation

It means, no special care to be given to a state at the expense of another state.

Principle of Transparency

It means, any country is prohibited to resort to quantitative limitations for protecting its national industry, but it can depend, if necessary, on tariffs.

Principle of Trade Negotiations

It means, the agreement's article and the GATT are the appropriate negotiation framework for the implementation of the provisions or the settlement of disputes.

Principle of the Preferential Transactions:

It means, the developing countries, taking their conditions into consideration, are given preferential transactions with the developed countries.

Principle of Reciprocity

It means, liberalization of international trade through multilateral negotiations on the basis of reciprocity, which implies that lifting of tariff barriers by any country should be met by equivalent lifting from the other country.

The Main GATT Agreements

The GATT Agreement includes 28 agreements in the following areas:

- Trade in textiles and ready made clothes
- Trade in agricultural goods
- Subsidy, dumping control and protection of domestic products
- Protection of intellectual property with respect to trade
- Environment and its relating with trade
- Measures of investments related with trade
- Government purchases
- Trade of services.

TRADE RELATED ASPECTS OF INTELLECTUAL PROPERTY RIGHTS (TRIPS)

Introduction

Despite the fact that the interest in intellectual property rights has started since relatively a long time through:

- Bern Agreement for the Protection of Literary Works, 1986
- Paris Agreement for the Protection of Industrial Property "Patents, Trademarks and Industrial Models", 1983
- Rome Agreement for the Protection of Artistic Performance and Production and the Broadcast, 1961
- Washington Agreement for the Protection of Intellectual Property and Integrated Circuits, 1989
- International Federations that organize international transaction in the field of property rights, such as "Paris Federation", "The Hague Federation etc.

Many countries (developed countries in particular) considered that all these agreements are not enough and lack clear criteria, rules and principles that can guarantee necessary protection of intellectual property rights related with trade, as well as the lack of effective provisions for the settlement of international disputes. As a result, many countries resorted to their national legislation or applied certain measurements in the field of dispute settlement, thus causing continuous problems and tensions between each other.

That is why negotiations concerning world trade has witnessed the submission of many proposals and projects in connection with intellectual property rights related with trade.

The emergence of Trade Related Aspects of Intellectual Property Rights (TRIPS) was the result of these negotiations. The TRIPS Agreement includes 73 articles covering all aspects of intellectual property rights related with products, commodities and trade. The general features of these articles are:

General Principles and Provisions (from article 1 to article 8)

These articles are connected with activities that serve development and technological progress so as to guarantee the realization of balance and the protection of other's rights

Areas of Protection (from article 9 to article 40) divided as follows:

- From article 9 to article 14: for the protection of copy right
- From article 15 to article 21: for the protection of trademarks
- From article 22 to article 24: for the protection of geographical indications
- From article 25 to article 26: for the protection of industrial models and designs
- From article 27 to article 34: for the protection of patents
- From article 35 to article 38: for the protection of integrated circuits
- Article 39: connected with industrial secrets (undisclosed information)
- Article 40: connected with measures to confront practices against competitiveness.

Measures for the Implementation of the Agreement (from article 41 to article 73), divided as follows:

- From article 41 to article 62: dealing with details of these measures
- From article 63 to article 64: dealing with settlement of disputes
- From article 65 to article 67: transitional arrangements and assistance given to developing countries by developed countries
- From item 68 to item 73: establishing arrangements and the agreements final provisions

All these 73 articles can be studied carefully, item by item, in order to be aware of means of its application and what are the necessary modifications that should be made in some of the domestic legislation related with intellectual property, in accordance with the GATT Agreement. These modifications should take into consideration the country's national interests in economic and industrial development, as well as the country's social conditions.

At present, the agreement has become a reality and entered into force since the first of January 1995 in all the member states, including the developing countries. Egypt, for example, is taking constitutional steps for ratifying the agreement, applying it and making necessary changes in some domestic legislation to be in conformity with its articles, including the articles and items related with intellectual property rights in the trade agreement.

In this respect, developing countries, including Egypt, should take into consideration the following points:

The accurate study of the agreement's articles and items, so as to have a clear vision and know exactly the measures that should be taken in the following areas:

- Obligations stipulated in the agreement items
- Modifications to be done in national legislation in the field of intellectual property, in conformity with the agreement.
- Minimizing the expected harms and maximizing the positive impacts
- Deep understanding of the agreement's items, and considering it the most important international legal instrument in modern history. Thus understanding the new situation, created by the agreement, that can affect the process of global economy in general, as well as the direct impact on the performance of national institutions for research and development.
- Get acquaintance with new rights and duties stipulated in the agreement. Changes should be introduced to national legislation to be in conformity with the agreement's item when it enters into force.
- Get acquaintance with the practices, allowed by the agreement, within the framework of new international legitimacy, even if implicitly or indirectly, and without stating clearly. These practices can be translated in the form of articles to be included in the new Egyptian Patent Law and its executive regulation.
- Get acquaintance with the available opportunities of attracting direct and indirect foreign investments, if abiding with what results from the new economic situation.

New constraints due to the agreement and, accordingly, its negative impacts, such as the following:

- *Expansion of the technological domain that need to be protected*: such as protection of products and processes of production in all technological fields; protection of innovations in the fields of chemical, pharmacological, pharmaceutical, nutritional and agricultural products, as well as the animal wealth, all of which are not protected in the current law no. 132 for the year 1949.
- *Expansion of the protection period for technology*: this means to increase the protection period to 20 years for patents. The current law provides with a protection period of only 15 years for all kinds of patents, and 10 years for processes of manufacturing chemical pharmacological and chemical nutritional and agricultural products.
- *Monopoly, by the patent owner to the rights of importing the products*: this means limitations on any foreign source to freely import the products under protection. The only way to prevent these harms is that the new Patent Law should stipulate the rights of the domestic parties to make use of the invention through its application in the field of production, which is known as obligatory license and in conformity with the agreement (article 31).

- *Protection of products obtained by using the protected processes of production*: this can be achieved through giving the owner of the patent, on the process of production, an exclusive concession an exclusive sale and to import the product which can be obtained directly through the process of production subject to protection.

  This does not prevent from parallel importing of other real goods that are not contradicting with other requirements stipulated in the GATT agreements. The parallel import helps in decreasing the prices and encouraging patent owners to apply their inventions in the industrial field in Egypt.

- *Expansion of the rights of the patent owner*: through providing patent owners with protection without any differentiation depending on the place or the technological subject of the invention, or whether the products are imported or produced nationally.

  This opens the door for all inventors (inside and outside Egypt) to enjoy protection.

  Against this constraint, the national industry can benefit from using the grace period stipulated in the agreement (article 65) for 5 years and additional 5 years for the products which are not protected in order to provide research and development institutions with the opportunities to change their policies and organizations in the face of this constraint.

RECOMMENDATIONS

Developing and modifying the national legislation in the field of protecting intellectual property, including the development of the Egyptian Patent Law, the Trademark and Industrial Designs Law, as to be in conformity with the agreement's articles and satisfy, in the same time, the national interests.

Developing and modifying the legislation related with foreign investment in Egypt, so as to attract new foreign technologies, especially from developed countries, to make use of them in scientific research and the development of the national industry in Egypt.

Giving due care to research, development and scientific institutions in the field of generating new technologies through national capacities. This can be achieved by getting rid of all difficulties in the road of progress.

Making use of the transitional arrangements stipulated in it. This can open opportunities for the national institutions to achieve self development in the face of the agreement's constraints, and in the same time not lose the opportunity of attracting foreign investment to Egypt.

1. Documentation Registration: Publication Department

- Receiving patent applications
- Controlling the payment of annual fees & publication fees

- Issuing patent & patent gazettes
- Preparing statistics

2. Technical Examination Department

- Examine patent applications
- Classify patent applications according to IPC system
- Search in the library for related patents to the subject

3. Legal Examination Department

- Legal examination represent the office in court
- Cases verifications
- Advice in legal cases.

4. Information Department (Library and Computer)

- Collect and arrange foreign patents and patent application from different countries such as GB, US, FR, EPO, WO, etc. on paper form, microforms and on CD-ROMS
- Store and retrieve bibliographic data and abstracts of the Egyptian patents and patent applications
- Prepare the state of-art searches with the assistance of the technical information department
- Design all type of data base and program use in the office
- Printing all information of official gazette

5. Technical Information and Technology Department

- Policy and planning
- International cooperation training
- State-of-the art searching
- Communications
- Preparing Egyptian patent abstracts
- Replying for the journalese

6. Administration Department

- Ddealing with personnel and finance matters
- The patent office has a relation with institutions and universities to help in examination patent applications whenever necessary and in particular field when thee is a lack of among the examiners in office.
- The relation of Egyptian patent office with WIPO especially in industrial property treaties is as follows.

Egypt is a Member:

- WIPO since 1975
- Paris convention since July 1, 1951
- Madrid agreement since July 1, 1952
- Hague agreement since July 1, 1952
- Strasbourg agreement since October 17, 1975
- TRIPS 1995

*** The Academy has a project for strengthening the patent office and its objectives are as follows:**

- Strengthening the patent office with regard to its structure, management & tasks
- Setting up with the patent office of:
  - ❖ Patent information and documentation services
  - ❖ A scheme for the promotion of local inventiveness
  - ❖ An examination and registration system for license contracts related to industrial property rights

As a result of the strengthening project the patent office is provided with:

- A mini-computer hp 3000 gx
- Ten terminals hp
- 4 CD-ROM work station
- Microfiche microfilm laboratory
- 3 photocopying machines
- Four reader-printer 2 canon-Minolta – 3M
- Now we have three CD-RI\OM work stations (3 computer hp one 286 and two 486)
- Three hp laser jet 4 plus.

5

INTELLECTUAL PROPERTY RIGHTS IN EGYPT

Mohamed Swellam

(Assistant Director, Science & Technology Centre, ASRT, Egypt)

EGYPTIAN PATENT OFFICE

It was established in 1951 by the laws 132 of 1951 and is now affiliated to the Academy of Scientific Research and Technology since 1971. The new law 82/2002 was published on 3/6/2002 and Regulation 1366 published on 16/8/2003, new protected areas were added to the new law (Utility Model, Layout Design & Integrated Circuit and Undisclosed Information).

EGYPT IS A MEMBER AT:

- WIPO since 1975
- Paris Convention since July 1, 1951
- Strasbourg agreement since October 17, 1975
- TRIPS agreement since 1995
- PCT agreement since 8/9/2003

GOALS OF PATENT OFFICE ACCORDING TO LAW

- Register patent application for the local and foreign inventions.
- Grant and issue patents to protect the ownership rights of the Egyptian and foreign inventors.
- Collect the foreign patent applications and arrange them to be easily accessible to examiners and users.

- Transfer the technological information from the patents all over the world and provide it to the specialists in order to develop their works and develop the local industries.
- Encourage inventors by helping them to participate in exhibitions and medals.
- Publish (monthly) the official patent gazette which includes filed, accepted application, granted patents, terminated applications and patents.

Organizational Structure

- Documentation Registration and Publication Department.
- Technical Examination Department.
- Legal Examination Department.
- Information Department (library and computer).
- Technical Information and Technology Department.
- Financial and Administrative Department.
- PCT Unit.

As a result of the strengthening project the patent office is provided with:

- Automation of the patent system for filing till granting Patent using a new WEB base database created and designed by the IT group of Egyptian Patent Office with cooperation of WIPO.
- Egyptian Patent Office website was launched since 2002 (www.egypo.gov.eg) and had mirrored on the WIPOnet since June 2003 (www.egypto.eg.wipo.net).

OFFICE LOCAL AREA NETWORK COMPRISES

- Five server one primary server, one Backup server, one database server, one for Archiving System and one Web server.
- More than 114 work stations.
- 18 network printers.
- Leased line (516K) for internet connection.

LAW 82/2002 AND REGULATION 1366/2003

- It was published on 3/6/2002 and 16/8/2003 respectively.
- It will protect new areas (Utility Model, Layout Design & Integrated Circuit and Undisclosed Information).
- The Law was harmonized according to TRIPS agreement and the pharmaceutical product will be protected at the end 2005.
- Novelty is international.

6

MANAGEMENT OF INTELLECTUAL PROPERTY RIGHTS IN INDIA

R. Saha

(Adviser, Department of Science and Technology and Director, Patent Facilitating Centre, Technology Information, Forecasting and Assessment Council, New Delhi, India)

INTRODUCTION

With the advent of the new knowledge economy, the old and some of the existing management constructs and approaches would have to change. The knowledge economy places a tag of urgency on understanding and managing knowledge based assets such as innovations and know-how. The time for grasping knowledge has become an important parameter for determining the success of an institution, enterprise, government and industry; the shorter the time better are the chances of success. Intellectual property rights (IPR) have become important in the face of changing trade environment which is characterized by the following features namely global competition, high innovation risks, short product cycle, need for rapid changes in technology, high investments in research and development (R&D), production and marketing and need for highly skilled human resources. Geographical barriers to trade among nations are collapsing due to globalisation, a system of multilateral trade and a new emerging economic order. It is therefore quite obvious that the complexities of global trade would be on the increase as more and more variables are introduced leading to uncertainties. Many products and technologies are simultaneously marketed and utilized in many countries. With the opening up of trade in goods and services intellectual property rights (IPR) have become more susceptible to infringement leading to inadequate return to the creators of knowledge. Developers of such products and technologies would like to ensure R&D costs and other costs associated with introduction of new products in the market are recovered and enough profits are generated for investing in R&D to keep up the R&D efforts.

One expects that a large number of IP rights would be generated and protected all over the world including India in all areas of science and technology, software and business methods.

More than any other technological area, drugs and pharmaceuticals match the above description most closely. Knowing that the cost of introducing a new drug into the market may cost a company anywhere between $ 300 million to $600 million along with all the associated risks at the developmental stage, no company will like to risk its intellectual property becoming a public property with out adequate returns. Creating, obtaining, protecting and managing intellectual property must become a corporate activity in the same manner as the raising of resources and funds. The knowledge revolution will demand a special pedestal for intellectual property and treatment in the overall decision- making process. It is also important to realize that each product is amalgamation of many different areas of science and technologies. In the face of the competition being experienced by the global community, many industries are joining hands for sharing their expertise in order to respond to market demands quickly and keeping the prices competitive. In order to maintain a continuous stream of new ideas and experimentations, public private partnership in R&D would need to be nurtured to arrive at a win-win situation. Therefore all publicly funded institutions and agencies will have to come to terms with the new ground realities and take positive steps to direct research suitably to generate more intellectual property rights, protect and manage them efficiently.

INTELLECTUAL PROPERTY RIGHTS (IPR)

Intellectual property rights as a collective term includes the following independent IP rights which can be collectively used for protecting different aspects of an inventive work for multiple protection:

- Patents
- Copyrights
- Trademarks
- Registered (industrial) design
- Protection of IC layout design
- Geographical indications, and
- Protection of undisclosed information

NATURE OF INTELLECTUAL PROPERTY RIGHTS

IPR are largely territorial rights except copyright, which is global in nature in the sense that it is immediately available in all the members of the Berne Convention. These rights are awarded by the State and are monopoly rights implying that no one can use these rights without the consent of the right holder. It is important to know that these rights have to be renewed from time to time for keeping them in force except in case of copyright and trade secrets. IPR have fixed term except trademark and geographical indications, which can have indefinite life, provided these are renewed after a stipulated time specified in the law by paying official fees. Trade secrets also have an infinite life but they don't have to be renewed. IPR can be assigned, gifted, sold and licensed like any other property. Unlike other moveable and immoveable properties, these rights can be simultaneously held in many countries at the same time. IPR can be held only by legal entities *i.e.*, who have the right to sell and purchase property. In other words an institution, which is not autonomous may not in a position to own an intellectual property. These rights especially, patents, copyrights, industrial designs, IC layout design and trade secrets are associated with something new or original and therefore, what is known in public domain cannot be protected through the rights mentioned above. Improvements and modifications made over known things can be protected. It would however, be possible to utilize geographical indications for protecting some agriculture and traditional products.

PATENTS

A patent is an exclusive right granted by a country to the owner of an invention to make, use, manufacture and market the invention, provided the invention satisfies certain conditions stipulated in the law. Exclusive right implies that no one else can make, use, manufacture or market the invention without the consent of the patent holder. This right is available for a limited period of time. In spite of the ownership of the rights, the use or exploitation of the rights by the owner of the patent may not be possible due to other laws of the country, which has awarded the patent. These laws may relate to health, safety, food, security etc. Further, existing patents in similar area may also come in the way. A patent in the law is a property right and hence, can be gifted, inherited, assigned, sold or licensed. As the right is conferred by the State, it can be revoked by the State under very special circumstances even if the patent has been sold or licensed or manufactured or marketed in the meantime. The patent right is territorial in nature and inventors/their assignees will have to file separate patent applications in countries of their interest, along with necessary fees, for obtaining patents in those countries. A new chemical process or a drug molecule or an electronic circuit or a new surgical instrument or a vaccine is a patentable subject matter provided all the stipulations of the law are satisfied.

The Indian Patent Act

The first Indian patent laws were first promulgated in 1856. These were modified from time to time. New patent laws were made after the independence in the form of the Indian Patent Act 1970. The Act has now been radically amended to become fully compliant with the provisions of TRIPS. The most recent amendments were made in 2005, which were preceded by the amendments in 2000 and 2003. While the process of bringing out amendments was going on, India became a member of the Paris Convention, Patent Cooperation Treaty and Budapest Treaty. The salient and important features of the amended Act are explained here.

Definition of Invention

A clear definition has now been provided for an invention, which makes it at par with definitions followed by most countries. Invention means a new product or process involving an inventive step and capable of industrial application. New invention means any invention or technology which has not been anticipated by publication in any document or used in the country or elsewhere in the world before the date of filing of patent application with complete specification *i.e.*, the subject matter has not fallen in public domain or it does not form part of the state of the art.

Inventive step means a feature of an invention that involves technical advance as compared to existing knowledge or having economic significance or both and that makes the invention not obvious to a person skilled in the art.

"Capable of industrial application means that the invention is capable of being made or used in an industry".

Novelty

An invention will be considered novel if it does not form a part of the global state of the art. Information appearing in magazines, technical journals, books, newspapers etc. constitutes the state of the art. Oral description of the invention in a seminar/ conference can also spoil novelty. Novelty is assessed in a global context. An invention will cease to be novel if it has been disclosed in the public through any type of publications anywhere in the world before filing a patent application in respect of the invention. Therefore it is advisable to file a patent application before publishing a paper if there is a slight chance that the invention may be patentable. Prior use of the invention in the country of interest before the filing date can also destroy the novelty. Novelty is determined through extensive literature and patent searches. It should be realized that patent search is essential and critical for ascertaining novelty as most of the information reported in patent documents does not get published anywhere else. For an invention to be novel, it need not be a major breakthrough. No invention is small or big. Modifications to the existing state of the art, process or product or both, can also be candidates for patents provided these were not earlier known. In a chemical process, for example, use of new reactants, use of a catalyst, new process conditions can lead to a patentable invention.

Inventiveness (Non-obviousness)

A patent application involves an inventive step if the proposed invention is not obvious to a person skilled in the art *i.e.*, skilled in the subject matter of the patent application. The prior art should not point towards the invention implying that the practitioner of the subject matter could not have thought about the invention prior to filing of the patent application. Inventiveness cannot be decided on the material contained in unpublished patents. The complexity or the simplicity of an inventive step does not have any bearing on the grant of a patent. In other words a very simple invention can qualify for a patent. If there is an inventive step between the proposed patent and the prior art at that point of time, then an invention has taken place. A mere 'scintilla' of invention is sufficient to found a valid patent. It may be often difficult to establish the inventiveness, especially in the area of up coming knowledge areas. The reason is that it would depend a great deal on the interpretative skills of the inventor and these skills will really be a function of knowledge in the subject area.

Usefulness

An invention must possess utility for the grant of patent. No valid patent can be granted for an invention devoid of utility. The patent specification should spell out various uses and manner of practicing them, even if considered obvious. If you are claiming a process, you need not describe the use of the compound produced thereby. Nevertheless it would be safer to do so. But if you claim a compound without spelling out its utility, you may be denied a patent.

Non Patentable Inventions

An invention may satisfy the conditions of novelty, inventiveness and usefulness but it may not qualify for a patent under the following situations:

1. An invention which is frivolous or which claims anything obviously contrary to well established natural laws *e.g.* different types of perpetual motion machines.
2. An invention whose intended use or exploitation would be contrary to public order or morality or which causes serious prejudice to human, animal or plant life or health or to the environment *e.g.*, a process for making brown sugar will not be patented.
3. The mere discovery of a scientific principal or formulation of an abstract theory *e.g.*, Raman effect and Theory of Relativity cannot be patented.
4. The mere discovery of a new form of a known substance which does not result in enhancement of the known efficacy of that substance or the mere discovery of any new property or new use of a known substance or the mere use of a known process, machine or apparatus unless such a known process results in a new product or employs at least one new reactant. For the purposes of this clause, salts, esters, polymorphs, metabolites, pure form, particle size, isomers, mixtures of isomers, complexes, combinations and other derivatives of known substance shall be considered to be the same substance unless they differ significantly in properties with regard to efficacy.
5. A substance obtained by a mere admixture resulting only aggregation of the properties of the components thereof or a process for producing such substance.
6. The mere arrangement or rearrangement or duplication of features of known devices each functioning independently of one another in a known way. If you put torch bulbs around an umbrella and operate them by a battery so that people could see you walking in rain when it is dark, then this arrangement is patentable as bulbs and the umbrella perform their functions independently.
7. A method of agriculture or horticulture. For example, the method of terrace farming cannot be patented.
8. Any process for medical, surgical, curative, prophylactic, diagnostic, therapeutic or other treatment of human beings, or any process for a similar treatment of animals to render them free of disease or to increase economic value or that of their products. For example, a new surgical technique for hand surgery for removing contractions is not patentable.
9. Inventions relating to atomic energy.
10. Discovery of any living thing or non-living substance occurring in nature.
11. Mathematical or business methods or a computer program per se or algorithms.

12. Plants and animals in whole or any part thereof other than microorganisms but including seeds, varieties and species and essentially biological processes for production and propagation of plants and animals.
13. A presentation of information.
14. Topography of integrated circuits.
15. A mere scheme or rule or method of performing mental act or method of playing games.
16. An invention which, in effect, is traditional knowledge or which is aggregation or duplication of known component or components.

Computer program per se as such has not been defined in the Act but would generally tend to mean that a computer program with out any utility would not be patentable. Protection of seeds and new plant varieties is covered under a different Act, which provides a protection for a period of 10 years. Similarly, topography of integrated circuits is protected through yet a different Act.

Term of the Patent

Term of the patent will be 20 years from the date of filing for all types of inventions.

Application

In respect of patent applications filed, following aspects will have to be kept in mind:

- Claim or claims can now relate to single invention or group of inventions linked so as to form a single inventive concept.
- Patent application will be published 18 months after the date of filing.
- Applicant has to request for examination 12 months within publication or 48 months from date of application, whichever is later.

No person resident in India shall, except under the authority of a written permit sought in the manner prescribed and granted by or on behalf of the Controller, make or cause to be made any application outside India for the grant of a patent for an invention unless (a) an application for a patent for the same invention has been made in India, not less than six weeks before the application outside India; and (b) either no direction has been given under the secrecy clause of the Act or all such directions have been revoked.

Provisional Specification

A provisional specification is usually filed to establish priority of the invention in case the disclosed invention is only at a conceptual stage and a delay is expected in submitting full and specific description of the invention. Although, a patent application accompanied with provisional specification does not confer any legal patent rights to the applicants, it is, however, a very important document to establish the earliest ownership of an invention. The provisional specification is a permanent and independent scientific cum legal document and no amendment is allowed in this. No patent is granted on the basis of a provisional specification. It has to be followed by a complete specification for obtaining a patent for the said invention. Complete specification must be submitted within 12 months of filing the provisional specification. This period can be extended by 3 months. It is not necessary to file an application with provisional specification before the complete specification. An application with complete specification can be filed right at the first instance.

Complete Specification

It may be noted that a patent document is a techno-legal document and it has to be finalized in consultation with an attorney. Submission of complete specification is necessary to obtain a patent. Contents of a complete specification would include the following:

1. Title of the invention.
2. Field to which the invention belongs
3. Background of the invention including prior art giving drawbacks of the known inventions & practices.
4. Complete description of the invention along with experimental results.
5. Drawings etc. essential for understanding the invention.
6. Claims, which are statements, related to the invention on which legal proprietorship is being sought. Therefore the claims have to be drafted very carefully.

Compulsory License

Any time after three years from date of sealing of a patent, application for compulsory license can be made provided.

1. Reasonable requirements of public have not been met.
2. Patented invention is not available to public at a reasonably affordable price.
3. Patented invention is not worked in India.

Among other things, reasonable requirements of public are not satisfied if working of patented invention in India on a commercial scale *is being prevented or hindered by importation* of patented invention.

Applicant's capability including risk taking, ability of the applicant to work the invention in public interest, nature of invention, time elapsed since sealing, measures taken by patentee to work the patent in India will be taken into account. In case of national emergency or other circumstances of extreme urgency or public non-commercial use or an establishment of a ground of anti competitive practices adopted by the patentee, the above conditions will not apply.

A patentee must disclose the invention in a patent document for anyone to practice it after the expiry of the patent or practice it with the consent of the patent holder during the life of the patent.

Patenting of Microbiological Inventions

The Indian Patent Act has now a specific provision in regard to patenting of microorganisms and microbiological processes. It is now possible to get a patent for a microbiological process and also products emanating from such processes.

As it is difficult to describe a microorganism on paper, a system of depositing strain of microorganisms in some recognized depositories was evolved way back in 1949 in USA. An international treaty called "Budapest Treaty" was signed in Budapest in 1973 and later on amended in 1980. India became a member of this Treaty, with effect from December 17, 2001. This is an international convention governing the recognition of deposits in officially approved culture collections for the purpose of patent applications in any country that is a party to this treaty. Because of the difficulties and virtual impossibility of reproducing a microorganism from a description of it in a patent specification, it is essential to deposit a strain in a culture collection centre for testing and examination by others.

An inventor is required to deposit the strain of a microorganism in a recognized depository, which assigns a registration number to the deposited microorganism. This registration number needs to be quoted in the patent application dealing with the microorganism. Obviously a strain of microorganism is required to be deposited before filing a patent application. It may be observed that this mechanism obviates the need of describing a microorganism in the patent application. Further, samples of strains can be obtained from the depository for further working on the patent. There are many international depositories in different countries such as ATCC, DSM etc. that are recognized under the Budapest Treaty. The Institute of Microbial Technology (IMTEC), Chandigarh is the first Indian depository set up under the Budapest Treaty.

Mail Box Provision

TRIPS requires that countries, not providing product patents in respect of pharmaceuticals and chemical inventions have to put in a mechanism for accepting product patent applications with effect from 1st January 1995. Such applications will only be examined for grant of patents, after suitable amendments in the national patent law have been made. This mechanism of accepting product patent applications is called the "mail box" mechanism. This system has been in force in India and now such applications are being taken up for examination.

Exclusive Marketing Right

TRIPS requires that member countries of the WTO not having provision in their laws for granting product patents in respect of drugs and agrochemical, must introduce Exclusive Marketing Rights (EMR) for such products, if the following criteria are satisfied:

1. A patent application covering the new drug or agrochemical should have been filed in any of the WTO member countries after 1 January 1995;
2. A patent on the product should have been obtained in any of the member countries (which provides for product patents in drugs and agrochemical) after 1 January 1995;

3. Marketing approvals for the product should have been obtained in any of the member countries;
4. A patent application covering the product should have been filed after 1 January 1995 in the country where the EMR is sought;
5. The applicant should apply seeking an EMR by making use of the prescribed form and paying requisite fee.

EMR is only a right for exclusive marketing of the product and is quite different from a patent right. It is valid up to a maximum period 5 years or until the time the product patent laws come into effect. The necessary amendment to: the Patents Act, 1970 came into force on 26 March 1999. The provision is applicable with retrospective effect from 1 January 1995. As per the 2005 amendments in the Patents Act, the provision of EMR is no longer required. However, these rights were awarded in India from time to time and there have been some litigations as well, where the courts came up with quick decisions.

Timing for Filing a Patent Application

Filing of an application for a patent should be completed at the earliest possible date and should not be delayed. An application filed with provisional specification, disclosing the essence of the nature of the invention helps to register the priority by the applicant. Delay in filing an application may entail some risks like (i) other inventors might forestall the first inventor by applying for a patent for the said invention, and (ii) there may be either an inadvertent publication of the invention by the inventor himself/herself or by others independently of him/her. Publication of an invention in any form by the inventor before filing of a patent application would disqualify the invention to be patentable. Hence, inventors should not disclose their inventions before filing the patent application. The invention should be considered for publication after a patent application has been filed. Thus, it can be seen that there is no contradiction between publishing an inventive work and filing of patent application in respect of the invention.

PROTECTING NEW PLANT VARIETY

New plant varieties can now be protected in India under the New Plant Variety and Farmers Rights Protection Act in 2001. New plant varieties cannot be protected through patents. However, the Act has not become operational as subsidiary legislation is yet to be put in place. India has enacted this act, which, in addition to meeting the technical features of UPOV, provides rights to farmers to use the seeds from their own crops for planting the next crop. Further, there are provisions for benefit sharing with farmers, penalty for marketing spurious propagation material and protecting extant varieties. There is a provision for protecting extant variety and farmers' varieties as well. The total period for protection is 10 years from the date of registration.

There are 5 main criteria to arrive at a decision whether a plant variety is really new or not. These are distinctiveness, uniformity, stability, novelty and denomination. The variety shall be deemed to be distinct if it is clearly distinct from any other variety whose existence is a matter of common knowledge at the time of filing of the application. The variety shall be deemed to be uniform if, subject to the variation that may be accepted from the particular features of its propagation, it is sufficiently uniform in its relevant characteristics. The variety shall be deemed to be stable if its relevant characteristics remain unchanged after repeated propagation or, in the case of a particular cycle of propagation at the end of each such cycle. The variety shall be deemed to be new if, at the date of filing of the application for breeders right, propagating or harvesting material of the variety has not been sold or otherwise disposed of to others, by or with the consent of the breeder for the purpose of exploitation of the variety. The variety shall be designated by a denomination, which will be its generic designation. The premise that the variety denomination must be its generic designation class for a requirement that 'denomination must enable the variety to be identified.

COPYRIGHTS

Copyright is a right, which is available for creating an original literary or dramatic or musical or artistic work. Cinematographic films including sound track and video films and recordings on discs, tapes, perforated roll or other devices are covered by copyrights. Computer programs and software are covered under literary works and are protected in India under copyrights. The Copyright Act, 1957 as amended in 1983, 1984, 1992, 1994 and 1999 governs the copyright protection in India. The total term of protection for literary work is the author's life plus sixty years. For cinematographic films, records, photographs, posthumous publications, anonymous publication, works of government and international agencies the term is 60 years from the beginning of the calendar year following the year in which the work was published. For broadcasting, the term is 25 years from the beginning of the calendar year following the year in which the broadcast was made.

Copyright gives protection for the expression of an idea and not for the idea itself. For example, many authors write textbooks on physics covering various aspects like mechanics, heat, optics etc. Even though these topics are covered in several books by different authors, each author will have a copyright on the book written by him/her, provided the book is not a copy of some other book published earlier. India is a member of the Berne Convention, an international treaty on copyright. Under this Convention, registration of copyright is not an essential requirement for protecting the right. It would; therefore, mean that the copyright on a work created in India would be automatically and simultaneously protected through copyright in all the member countries of the Berne Convention. The moment an original work is created, the creator starts enjoying the copyright. However, an undisputable record of the date on which a work was created must be kept. When a work is published with the authority of the copyright owner, a notice of copyright may be placed on publicly distributed copies. The use of copyright notice is optional for the protection of literary and artistic works. It is, however, a good idea to incorporate a copyright notice. As violation of copyright is a cognizable offence, the matter can be reported to a police station. It is advised that registration of copyright in India would help in establishing the ownership of the work. The registration can be done at the Office of the Registrar of Copyrights in New Delhi. It is also to be noted that the work is open for public inspection once the copyright is registered.

Computer program in the Copyright Act has been defined as a set of instructions expressed in words, codes, schemes or any other form, including a machine-readable medium, capable of causing a computer to perform a particular task or achieve a particular result. It is obvious that algorithms, source codes and object codes are covered in this definition. It is advisable to file a small extract of the computer program at the time of registration rather than the full program. It is important to know that the part of the program that is not being filed, would remain a trade secret of the owner but would have to be kept well guarded by the owner. It may be noted that computer programs will become important in the area of medicines when one talks about codification of DNA and gene sequencing. Generally, all copyrightable expressions embodied in a computer program, including screen displays, are protectable. However, unlike a computer program, which is a literary work, screen display is considered an artistic work and therefore cannot be registered through the same application as that covering the computer program. A separate application giving graphical representation of all copyrightable elements of the screen display is essential. In the digital era, copyright is assuming a new importance as many works transacted through networks such as databases, multi media work, music, information etc. are presently the subject matter of copyright.

Coverage Provided by Copyright

1. Literary, dramatic and musical work. Computer programs/software are covered within the definition of literary work.
2. Artistic work.
3. Cinematographic films, which include sound track and video films.
4. Recording on any disc, tape, perforated roll or other device.

Infringement of Copyright

Copyright gives the creator of the work the right to reproduce the work, make copies, translate, adapt, sell or give on hire and communicate the work to public. Any of these activities done without the consent of the author or his assignee is considered infringement of the copyright. There is a provision of 'fair use' in the law, which allows copyrighted work to be used for teaching and research and development. In other words making one photocopy of a book for teaching students may not be considered an infringement, but making many photocopies for commercial purposes would be considered an infringement. There is one associated right with copyright, which is known as the 'moral right', which cannot be transferred and is not limited by the term. This right is enjoyed by the creator for avoiding obscene representation of his/her works. Following acts are considered infringement of copyrights:

1. In the case of **literary, dramatic or musical work**, not being a computer program:
   (*a*) To reproduce the work in any material form including the storing of it in any medium by electronic means;
   (*b*) To issue copies of the work to the public not being copies already in circulation;

(*c*) To perform the work in public, or communicate it to the public;

(*d*) To make any cinematography film or sound recording in respect of the work;

(*e*) To make any translation of the work; to make any adaptation of the work;

(*f*) To do, in relation to a translation or an adaptation of the work, any of the acts specified in relation to the work in Sub-clauses (1) to (4);

2. In the case of **computer program**:

(*a*) To do any acts specified in clauses (1);

(*b*)To sell or give on hire, or offer for sale or hire any copy of the computer program, regardless of whether such copy has been sold or given on hire on earlier occasions;

3. In the case of an **artistic work**:

(*a*) To reproduce the work in any material form including depiction in three dimensions of a two dimensional work or in two dimensions of a three dimensional work;

(*b*) To communicate the work to the public;

(*c*) To issue copies of the work to the public not being copies already in circulation;

(*d*) To include the work in any cinematography film;

(*e*) To make any adaptation of the work;

(*f*) To do, in relation to a translation or an adaptation of the work, any of the acts specified in relation to the work in sub-clauses (1) to (4);

4. In the case of a **cinematography film**:

(*a*) To make a copy of the film including a photograph of any image forming part thereof;

(*b*) To sell or give on hire or offer for sale or hire, any copy of the film, regardless of whether such copy has been sold or given on hire on earlier occasions;

(*c*) To communicate the film to the public;

5. In the case of **sound recording**:

(*a*) To make any other sound recording embodying it;

(*b*) To sell or give on hire or offer for sale or hire, any copy of the, sound recording, regardless of whether such copy has been sold or given on hire on earlier occasions;

(*c*) To communicate the sound recording to the public.

Explanation: For the purpose of this section, a copy that has been sold once shall be deemed to be a copy already in circulation.

Computer Program

A Computer includes any electronic or similar device having information processing capabilities. Computer program means a set of instructions expressed in words, codes, schemes or any other form, including a machine-readable medium, capable of causing a computer to perform a particular task or achieve a particular result. It is now possible to have copyrights both on object code and source code. Generally, all copyrightable expressions embodied in a computer program, including screen displays, are protectable. However, unlike a computer program, which is a literary work, screen displays are artistic work and cannot therefore be registered in the same application as that covering the computer program. A separate application giving graphic representation of all copyrightable elements of the screen display is necessary.

In the case of a program made in the course of author's employment under a contract of service or apprenticeship, the employer shall, in the absence of any agreement to the contrary, be the first owner of the copyright. However, works created by third parties on commission do not automatically vest the copyright in the commissioning party. If the third party is an independent contractor, it is essential for the commissioning party to obtain the copyright through a written deed of assignment. It is a common misconception that the copyright automatically belongs to the commissioning party. Thus, it is only where the developer is an employee creating the work under a contract of service that the rights belong to the employer.

Special Provisions for Computer Programs

Following tasks will not be considered infringement as they are legally allowed under the Indian laws:

The doing of any act necessary to obtain information essential for operating inter-operability of an independently created computer program with other programs by a lawful possessor of a computer program provided that such information is not otherwise readily available.

1. The observation, study or test of functioning of the computer program in order to determine the ideas and principles which underline any elements of the program while performing such acts necessary for the functions for which the computer program was supplied;
2. The making of copies or adaptation of the computer program from a personally legally obtained copy for non-commercial personal use.

One of the important requirements of copyright is that the work/expression should be fixed in a tangible medium for copyright protection. Protection attaches automatically to an eligible work of authorship, the moment the work is sufficiently fixed. A work is fixed when it is sufficiently permanent or stable to permit it to be perceived, reproduced, or otherwise communicated for a period of more than a transitory duration. A work may be fixed in words, numbers, notes, sounds, pictures, or any other graphic or symbolic indicia; may be embodied in a physical object in written, printed, photographic, sculptural, punched, magnetic, or any other stable form; and may be capable of perception either directly or by means of any machine or device now known or later developed. Basically, the fixation of a work should allow perceiving, reproducing, or communicating the work either directly or thorough some machine. For instance, floppy disks, compact discs (CDs), CD-ROMs, optical disks, compact discs-interactive (CDIs), digital tape, and other digital storage devices are all stable forms in which works may be fixed and from which works may be perceived, reproduced or communicated by means of a machine or device.

A simultaneous fixation (or any other fixation) meets the requirements if its embodiment in a copy or phonogram record is "sufficiently permanent or stable to permit it to be perceived, reproduced, or otherwise communicated for a period of more than transitory duration. "Works are not sufficiently fixed if they are "purely evanescent or transient" in nature, "such as those projected briefly on a screen, shown electronically on a television or cathode ray tube, or captured momentarily in the 'memory' of a computer." Electronic network transmissions from one computer to another, such as e-mail, may only reside on each computer in RAM (random access memory), but that has been found to be sufficient fixation.

Transfer of Copyright

The owner of the copyright in an existing work or prospective owner of the copyright in a future work may assign to any person the copyright, either wholly or partially in the following manner:

1. For the entire world or for a specific country or territory; or
2. For the full term of copyright or part thereof; or
3. Relating to all the rights comprising the copyright or only part of such rights.

INDUSTRIAL DESIGN

We see so many varieties and brands of the same product (*e.g.* car, television, personal computer, a piece of furniture etc.) in the market, which look quite different from each other. If the products have similar functional features or have comparable price tags, the eye appeal or visual design of a product determines the choice. Even if the similarities are not close, a person may decide to go for a more expensive item because that item has a better look or colour scheme. What is being said is that the external design or colour scheme or ornamentation of a product plays a key role in determining the market acceptability of the product over other similar products. If you have a good design that gives you an advantage, then you must have a system to protect its features otherwise there would be wide scale imitation.

Design as per the Indian Act means the features of shape, configuration, pattern, ornament or composition of lines or colours applied to any article - whether in two dimensional or three dimensional or in both forms - by any industrial process or means, whether manual, mechanical or chemical, separate or combined, which in the finished article appeal to and are judged solely by the eye; but it does not include any mode or principle of construction or anything which is in substance a mere mechanical device. In this context an article means any article of manufacture and any substance, artificial, or partly artificial and partly natural; and includes any part of an article capable of being made and sold separately. Stamps, labels, tokens, cards, etc cannot be considered an article for the purpose of registration of design because once the alleged design *i.e.*, ornamentation is removed only a piece of paper, metal or like material remains and the article referred to ceases to exist. An article must have its existence independent of the designs applied to it. So, the design as applied to an article should be integral with the article itself.

The Essential Requirements for the Registration of Design

1. The design should be new or original, not previously published or used in any country before the date of application for registration. The novelty may reside in the application of a known shape or pattern to a new subject matter. However, if the design for which the application is made does not involve any real mental activity for conception, then registration may not be considered.
2. The design should relate to features of shape, configuration, pattern or ornamentation applied or applicable to an article. Thus, designs of industrial plans, layouts and installations are not registrable under the Act.
3. The design should be applied or applicable to any article by any industrial process. Normally, designs of artistic nature such as painting, sculptures and the like which are not produced in bulk by any industrial process are excluded from registration under the Act.
4. The features of the designs in the finished article should appeal to and are judged solely by the eye. This implies that the design must appear and should be visible on the finished article, for which it is meant. Thus, any design in the inside arrangement of a box, money purse or almirah may not be considered for showing such articles in the open state, as those articles are generally put in the market in the closed state.
5. Any mode or principle of construction or operation or any thing, which is in substance a mere mechanical device, would not be a registrable design. For instance, a key having its novelty only in the shape of its corrugation or bend at the portion intended to engage with levers inside the lock it is associated with, cannot be registered as a design under the Act. However, when any design suggests any mode or principle of construction or mechanical or other action of a mechanism, a suitable disclaimer in respect thereof is required to be inserted on its representation, provided there are other registrable features in the design.
6. The design should not include any trademark or property mark or artistic works.
7. It should be significantly distinguishable from known designs or combination of known designs.
8. It should not comprise or contain scandalous or obscene matter.

Duration of the Registration of a Design

The total term of a registered design is 15 years. Initially the right is granted for a period of 10 years, which can be extended, by another 5 years by making an application and by paying a fee of Rs. 2000/- to the Controller before the expiry of initial 10 years period. The proprietor of design may make the application for such extension even as soon as the design is registered.

Strategy for Protection

First to file rule is applicable for registrability of design. If two or more applications relating to an identical or a similar design are filed on different dates, the first application will be considered for registration of design. Therefore the application should be filed as soon as you are ready with the design. After publication in the official gazette on payment of the prescribed fee of Rs. 500/- all registered designs are open for public inspection. Therefore, it is advisable to inspect the register of designs to determine whether the design is new or not. There is yet another important provision for ensuring that the design is different from anything published any where in the world. This is quite a strict condition. There would be many designs, which are not protected, and these would not be part of any database maintained by design offices. An applicant has to take the responsibility of ensuring that he has done an extensive search and satisfied himself of the novelty of his design. However, in practice as the cost involved in filing and obtaining a design registration is not high, a design application is made if the stakes involved are not high and you have not copied any design. The application for registration of design can be filed by the applicant himself or through a professional person (*i.e.* patent agent, legal practitioner etc.). An agent residing in India has to be employed by the applicants not resident of India.

TRADEMARKS

A trademark is a distinctive sign, which identifies certain goods or services as those produced or provided by a specific person or enterprise. Trademarks may be one or combination of words, letters, and numerals. They may also consist of drawings, symbols, three-dimensional signs such as shape and packaging of goods, or colours used as distinguishing feature. Collective marks are owned by an association whose members use them to identify themselves with a level of quality. Certification marks are given for compliance with defined standards. (Example ISO 9000.). A trademark provides to the owner of the mark by ensuring the exclusive right to use it to identify goods or services, or to authorize others to use it in return for some consideration (payment).

Well-known trademark in relation to any goods or services, means a mark which has become so to the substantial segment of the public which uses such goods or receives such services that the use of such mark in relation to other goods or services would be likely to be taken as indicating a connection in the course of trade or rendering of services between those goods or services and a person using the mark in relation to the first-mentioned goods or services.

Enactment of the Indian Trademarks Act 1999 is a big step forward from the Trade and Merchandise Marks Act 1958 and the Trademark Act 1940. The newly enacted Act has some features not present in the 1958 Act and these are:

1. Registration of service marks, collective marks and certification trademarks.
2. Increasing the period of registration and renewal from 7 years to 10 years.
3. Allowing filing of single application for registration in more than one class.

4. Enhanced punishment for offences related to trademarks.
5. Exhaustive definitions for terms frequently used.
6. Simplified procedure for registration of registered users and enlarged scope of permitted use.
7. Constitution of an Appellate Board for speedy disposal of appeals and rectification of applications, which at present lie before High Court.

Well-known Trademarks and Associated Trademarks

A well-known trademark in relation to any goods or services means a mark, which has become known to the substantial segment of the public that uses such goods or receives such services. Associated Trademarks are, in commercial terms, marks that resemble each other and are owned by the same owner, but are applied to the same type of goods or services. For example, a company dealing in readymade garments may use associated marks for shirts, trousers etc. means trademarks deemed to be, or required to be, registered as associated trademarks under this Act.

Service Marks

The Indian Act of 1958 did not have any reference to service marks. Service means service of any description that is made available to potential users and includes the provision of services in connection with the business of industrial or commercial matters such as banking, communication, education, financing, insurance, chit funds, real estate, transport, storage, material treatment, processing, supply of electrical or other energy, boarding, lodging, entertainment, amusement, construction, repair, conveying of news or information and advertising. Marks used to represent such services are known as service marks.

Certification Trademarks and Collective Marks

A certification trade mark means a guarantee mark which indicates that the goods to which it is applied are of a certain quality or are manufactured in a particular way or come from a certain region or use some specific material or maintain a certain level of accuracy. The goods must originate from a certain region rather from a particular trader. Certification marks are also applicable to services and the same parameters will have to be satisfied. Further these marks are registrable just like any other trademark. Agmark used in India for various food items is a kind of certification mark although it is not registered as a certification mark; the concept of certification mark was not in vogue at the time of introduction of Agmark.

A collective mark means a trademark distinguishing from those of others, the goods or services of members of an association of persons (not being a partnership within the meaning of the Indian Partnership Act, 1932), which is the proprietor of the mark.

Term of a Registered Trademark

The initial registration of a trademark shall be for a period of ten years but may be renewed from time to time for an unlimited period by payment of the renewal fees.

PROTECTION OF GEOGRAPHICAL INDICATIONS

Indications which identify a good as originating in the territory of a member or a region or a locality in that territory, where a given quality reputation or other characteristics of the good is attributable to its geographical origin. The concept of identifying GI and protecting them is a new concept in India, perhaps in most developing countries, and has come to knowledge in these countries after they signed the TRIPS Agreement. It may be noted that properly protected GI will give protection in domestic and international market. Stipulations of TRIPS would be applicable to all the member countries. According to TRIPS, GI which is not or cease to be protected in its country of origin or which has fallen into disuse in that country cannot be protected. Homonymous GI for wines will get independent protection. Each state shall determine conditions under which homonymous indications will be differentiated from each other. Principles of national treatment and fair competition are applicable. TRIPS provide for seizure of goods bearing false indications of GI. TRIPS provide for refusal or invalidation of registration of a trademark containing a GI with respect to goods not originating in the territory indicated. The Geographical Indication of Goods (Registration and Protection) Act came into being in 2000. (The Act is not implemented at the time of writing the article, as the rules have not been notified.)

The term GI has been defined as "Geographical Indications", in relation to goods, means an indication which identifies such goods as agricultural goods, natural goods or manufactured goods as originating, or manufactured in the territory of a country, or a region or locality in that territory, where a given quality, reputation or other characteristics of such goods is essentially attributable to its geographical origin and in case where such goods are manufactured goods one of the activities of either the production or of processing or preparation of thc goods concerned takes place in such territory, region or locality, as the case may be.

Applicants for GI's Tegistration

Any association of persons or producers or any organization or authority established by or under any law for the time being in force representing the interest of the producers of the concerned goods, who are desirous of registering geographical indication in relation to such goods shall apply in writing to the Registrar in such form and in such manner and accompanied by such fees as may be prescribed for the registration of the geographical indication.

Non-registrable Geographical Indications

Geographical indications having following cannot be registered:

1. The use of which would be likely to deceive or cause confusion or contrary to any law.
2. Which comprises or contains scandalous or obscene matter or any matter likely to hurt religion susceptibility of any class or section of citizens of India.

3. Which would other wise is disentitled to protection in a court.
4. Which are determined to be generic names or indications of goods and are, therefore, not or ceased to be protected in their country of origin or which have fallen into disuse in that Country.
5. Which, although literally true as to the territory, region or locality in which the goods originate, but falsely represent to the persons that the goods originate in another territory, region or locality, as the case may be.

Punishment for Falsifying GI

A sentence of imprisonment for a term between six months to three years and a fine between fifty thousand rupees and two lakh rupees is provided in the Act. The court may reduce the punishment under special circumstances.

Term of GI Protection

The registration of a GI shall be for a period of ten years but may be renewed from time to time for an unlimited period by payment of the renewal fees.

PROTECTION OF INTEGRATED CIRCUIT LAYOUT DESIGN (IC)[7]

It provides protection for semiconductor IC layout designs. India has now in place Semiconductor Integrated Circuits Layout Design Act, 2000 to give protection to IC layout design. Layout design includes a layout of transistors and other circuitry elements and includes lead wires connecting such elements and expressed in any manner in a semiconductor IC. Semiconductor IC is a product having transistors and other circuitry elements, which are inseparably formed on a semiconductor material or an insulating material or inside the semiconductor material and designed to perform an electronic circuitry function. The term of the registration is 10 years from the date of filing.

An IC layout design cannot be registered if it is:

1. Not original;
2. Commercially exploited anywhere in India or in a convention country;
3. Inherently not distinctive;
4. Inherently not capable of being distinguishable from any other registered layout design.

Note: Design not exploited commercially for more than 2 years from date of registration of application shall be treated as commercially exploited for the purpose of this Act.

Reproducing, importing, selling, distributing the IC layout design for commercial purposes only constitutes infringement. A person when creates another layout design on the basis of scientific evaluation of a registered layout design shall not be causing any infringement.

PROTECTION OF UNDISCLOSED INFORMATION

The protected subject matter is information lawfully within the control of a natural person or legal person that is secret that has commercial value because it is secret and that has been subject to reasonable steps by the person lawfully in control of the information, to keep it secret. Secret is defined as " secret in the sense that it is not, as a body or in the precise configuration and assembly of its components known among or readily accessible to persons within the circles that normally deal with the kind of information in question." Undisclosed information, generally known as trade secret/confidential information, includes formula, pattern, compilation, programme, device, method, technique or process. Protection of undisclosed information is least known to players of IPR and also least talked about, although it is perhaps the most important form of protection for industries, R&D institutions and other agencies dealing with IPRs. Protection of undisclosed information/trade secret is not really new to humanity; at every stage of development people have evolved methods to keep important information secret, commonly by restricting the knowledge to their family members. Laws relating to all forms of IPR are at different stages of implementation in India, but there is no separate and exclusive law for protecting undisclosed information/trade secret or confidential information. The Contract Act of 1872 would however cover many aspects of trade secrets.

It is difficult to define the term in its entirety but, for an easy understanding, it may be said that a piece of undisclosed information or a trade secret can be as simple an item as a company's customer list or as complex as a formula for a product or a process. Broadly speaking, the term would encompass information, including a formula, pattern, compilation, program, device, method, technique or process that provides the owner with an advantage over his business competitors who do not know or use it and is of significance or importance to the business of the company holding the information. Expanding it further, it may include new product plans, product costing, best material to use, sources of materials, financial standing of the business, accounting information, employee records, credit rating of customers, production information, manufacturing methods and processes, business methods, blueprints, test data, research reports, professional pollsters, technical drawings and organisational structure, specifications, process manuals, written instructions for operating the process and analytical means to check and control the product and processes, details of workshop practice, technical training and personal visitation and inspection. On the software side it would include source code, the data file structure, the structure sequence and organisation of computer program. It may also include information relating to a patented invention not included in the patent specification, inventions capable of being patented but not patented, inventions incapable of being patented in a particular country because of the subject matter being excluded in the patent law of that country, inventions incapable of being patented by reason of lack of inventiveness, industrial designs capable of being registered but not registered, industrial designs having functional characteristics and skills, experience and craftsmanship of technicians. The information can be intangible and invisible as well and can take myriad forms, and therefore, any attempt to define it in an exhaustive manner would be practically meaningless.

A trade secret is a valuable piece of information with the essential requirement that the information be treated as such, *i.e.* as a secret. The value of a trade secret resides in the fact that competitors or other interested parties do not have access to it. Therefore, a trade secret must be kept secret so that no one could, with out the consent of the owner, acquire it. Trade secrecy is basically a do-it-yourself form of protection. You do not register with the government to secure your trade secrets. *The only way to acquire it with out the consent of the owner would be through devious or unlawful means.* The owner has the exclusive right to use/exploit a trade secret as long as it remains a secret. As a result, theoretically speaking, the term of a trade secret could be indeterminate or infinite. It is said that the trade secret of Coca-Cola still has not entered the public domain despite the fact that the common ingredients of Coca-Cola are known. A chemical composition falling in this category need to be protected through a trade secret rather than patent which is a publicly known document. It is usually said that the term of the trade secret relating to a machine tool is only as long as the company keeps it internal secret. The moment the product is in the market, many people will know how to copy the product and the moment the product is copied the trade secret associated with the copied aspects will no longer remain valid and secret, hence the protection will be lost and the term of the protection will be over. By and large this would be true for design features but trade secret can be maintained about say, composition of materials used and the process conditions adopted for manufacturing.

OTHER RELATED LEGISLATION

India enacted the Biodiversity Act 2002 to ensure maintenance, sustenance and development of its biodiversity. The Act has specific provisions about ownership of intellectual property rights associated with exploitation of biodiversity. Industries have to have the prior informed consent of the National Biodiversity Authority before exploring the biodiversity in India. In the event of R&D based on exploitation of biodiversity and associated local knowledge, there is a provision for sharing of benefits of such work with the local community. No direct flow of funds is expected to the community. In stead the Union Government will reach the benefits through State Governments to the community.

The other Act having its influence over other Acts related to IPR is the Information technology Act, 2000 which looks at the security aspect of material being transacted on internet.

MANAGEMENT OF IPR IN PUBLICLY FUNDED INSTITUTIONS IN INDIA

Aims of publicly funded institutions such as universities, colleges, autonomous bodies and public sector undertakings are multifaceted and are not purely driven by economic considerations but they are primarily driven by considerations of social obligations and political objectives and will of a nation. India has stuck to these aims since the independence. On one hand the above approach has helped us in creating a pool of highly educated population and also building an inherent strength in research and development and core competency in basic industries like steel, power, fertilizers etc. However on the other hand, an insulated system breeds complacency, which blunts the spirit of innovation and fire for being ahead of others. Globalization has taught us many new lessons by opening our eyes to the existing and forthcoming ground realities, which cannot be shunned away just because we do not happen to like them. These realities are going to stay. The likely impacts of globalization started becoming a part of our age old thought process and life style when India decided to become a member of the World Trade Organization. Since the beginning of 1990s new approaches started taking roots in respect of such institutions, especially related to their management and source of funding. It has been observed that educational and R&D institutions are being asked to generate their own funds and depend less and less on block grants by central or state governments. In respect of PSU the message has been to generate more and more revenue from the available resources. The Central Government was quick to understand the importance of innovations and new ideas for adjusting to new streams of paradigm shifts. The Government also realized that the journey is not going to be smooth, easy or straight forward in the absence of knowledge about new paradigms among scientists, technologists and policy makers. January 1, 1995 came and brought with it the full impact of WTO along with the Agreement of Trade Related Aspects of Intellectual Property Rights (TRIPS). The Indian system rose to the new challenge and through its many efforts have taken successful steps towards transition to a new culture by updating its existing laws, enacting new legislations, instituting new mechanisms for enabling creation of new intellectual property and its protection and even evolving novel methods and schemes to promote innovations at grass roots levels. Managing creativity within the innovation process is not easy. From providing initial impetus for new ideas and a means of collating and evaluating them through to determining the most appropriate exploitation strategy and selecting delivery partners, innovation is a process and can therefore be managed.

Indian S&T Scenario

The national expenditure on Research and Development (R&D) in India increased from Rs. 8913.61 crores in 1996-97 to Rs. 12901.54 crores in 1998-99. The projected R&D expenditure would reach a level of about Rs. 15090.22 crores in 1999-2000 and Rs. 17660.21 crores in 2000-2001. The share of the various sectors in the total R&D expenditure in 1998-99 was - Central Government including public sector industry contributed 67.5%, private sector 21.6%, State governments 8.0% and the higher education sector 2.9%.

The R&D expenditure as a percentage of GNP was 0.81% as compared to 0.79% in 1990-91. Though in absolute terms the R&D expenditure has shown an increasing trend, the R&D expenditure as a percentage of GNP has hovered around 0.8%. The projected R&D expenditure as percentage of GNP in 1999-2000 and 2000-2001 are 0.87% and 0.94% respectively. It may be noted that in the coming years, the R&D expenses by the education sector is likely to go up as the academic institutions interact more and more with the industry and are thereby motivated to spend their own resources in R&D. As greater awareness about protecting intellectual property gets generated in industry and academics, contract research would necessarily be driven by the need to generate, protect and manage IPR. This trend will leverage more funds in R&D and improve the return from investment in R&D.

The national R&D expenditure by objectives in 1998-99 was in the following areas in order of the share of the expenditure, agriculture forestry and fishing, defence, space, promotion of industrial development, development of health services, energy, general advancement of knowledge, transport and communication and environment. It may be noted that majority of funding for R&D comes from the Government and is carried out in publicly funded institutions. Therefore the role of the government in capacity building in management of IPR is fundamental and of utmost importance.

Capacity Building

Experts who have been involved in capacity building in different areas would agree that the exercise of capacity building is never monolithic in nature but a multidimensional and complex activity. No exercise at a national level can succeed if all or most players are not engaged in the activity. Intellectual Property Rights are often considered synonym of patents or at best patents, trademark and copyrights. This type of understanding or misunderstanding may be present elsewhere in the world. Sometimes people even use the word 'patent' as a substitute for 'protect'. Lets not forget that India is a big country and the task of spreading literacy is gigantic Dissemination of new knowledge is difficult and it cannot be disseminated in a day or two; hence one should be prepared to work with low success rates. At the same time the need to make efforts for spreading correct literacy in a short period of time cannot be overlooked. Awareness still remains an unfulfilled goal in spite of efforts made by so many agencies. There is a need to adopt different means such as contact programmes, print media, bulletins, internet, videos etc. Awareness by itself is of little use if the State does not create and provide suitable systems to enable scientists, technologists, industries and even the State to protect their rights. These means would be in terms of technical guidance, financial support, legal help and other facilitation steps. If you teach scientists that novelty is one of the key factors for getting a patent and do not supply them with adequate tools to determine if their inventions are novel or not, the awareness will have be of little value. Universities in India are very poor and their management systems are very old. Therefore, they need technical, financial and legal help to move ahead; someone has to hold their hands.

Capacity building has to be multifaceted at the national level in order to move and remain ahead in the knowledge race. Academic institutions, R&D institutions, industries (goods and services), government departments and ministries (law making, regulating, providing funds and incentives for research etc) and other agencies, attorney firms, courts and NGOs need to be enabled and empowered for playing a constructive role in the process of capacity building. Policy frameworks are essential in the national context to give the right impetus to the activities already started and also provide a broad platform for taking up future activities. Many of these issues have been addressed and addressed quite successfully in the last ten years by different agencies of the government. While departments like Atomic Energy, Space and DRDO and agencies like CSIR have their in house system for looking after their needs of IPR, There was no agency in the country in 1995, which could cut across departments and agencies and become a national nodal point for information and advice on IPR.

Patent Facilitating Centre (PFC)

The Department of Science and Technology set up the Patent Facilitating Centre at the Technology Information Forecasting and Assessment Council (TIFAC) in 1995 as a small initiative to address the need of awareness creation among scientists, helping them to protect their inventive and original work through IP laws and also act as a watch dog. The PFC came to be known for its capability to raise issues and bringing new information and knowledge about IPR in public domain. Starting with the revelation of the turmeric patent to the whole country, it brought to notice many other patents using some of our well-known plants and traditional knowledge and, at times, claiming what is already known in India. The days of Dunkel Draft on WTO became a history with PFC putting IPR matters in public domain freely through its monthly IPR Bulletin since November 1995 (now it is available on the net). The readership of these bulletins is over 10000. These bulletins cover technical analysis of granted patents, case laws, current global issues, IPR laws of India and other countries, international treaties, analysis of patents tends, domestic and international news and many other items of interest to a wide variety of readers.

The PFC has organized 275 IPR awareness workshops all over the country independently and also in association with Ministry of Small Scale Industries, Department of Atomic Energy, Department of Space and ICMR. In the process almost 30000 scientists, technologists and policy makers have been sensitized from about 500 universities, colleges and R&D institutions and 800 industries. The PFC has been organizing advanced level of training programmes with CII and attorney firms and also workshops cum retreat on topics such as public private partnership in IPR management. It would be pertinent to mention at this point that the Ministry of Human Resource Development (MHRD) has also been supporting workshops on IPR. Further, the MHRD has created 11 IPR chairs in various IITS and universities. The Ministry of Commerce and Industry has also been conducting many seminars and workshops on this topic for the last decade or so. As mentioned earlier, these efforts have to be supplemented with some hardcore products and processes to lead to logical conclusions/output. Indian patent data was not available in a searchable digital form. People in the field realize that it is almost impossible to search for patents from the gazette. The PFC brought out Ekaswa A and Ekaswa B databases on the patent applications filed in India and the patent applications accepted by the Patent Office. These are available on the Internet as well and are being used extensively by industries.

Twenty Patent Information Centres (PIC) have been set up by the PFC in 20 States namely; Assam, Andhra Pradesh, Chattisgarh, Goa, Gujarat, Haryana, Himachal Pradesh, Jammu and Kashmir, Karnataka, Kerala, Madhya Pradesh, Manipur, Punjab, Rajasthan, Sikkim, Tamil Nadu, Tripura, Uttar Pradesh, Uttranchal and West Bengal. These PICs are helping scientists, technologists and policy makers in their respective States by creating awareness and extending help for protecting their inventions. Some States as a result of continuous discussions have filed applications for registration of some products as geographical indications; some are also in the pipeline. Two PICs, namely, Punjab and West Bengal, have also succeeded in introducing IPR courses in technical institutions; other PICs are working hard towards this goal.

The PFC is the only window available in the country, which provides full technical, legal and financial support for inventions emanating from educational institutions, including schools and colleges, and government departments. It has so far filed 260 patent applications in India and other countries from about 55 universities/academic institutions and many of them have been granted.

Other Centres/Cells

Many government departments, educational institutions and PSU have started their IPR cells. Prominent among the government departments/agencies are Department of Biotechnology, Ministry of Telecommunications and Information Technology, Indian Council of Medical Research, Indian Council of Agricultural Research, ISRO, Department of Atomic Energy, Defence Research and Development Organization and Indian Council of Forest Research. IITs at Delhi, Mumbai, Kharagpur and Roorkee have also set up their cells and evolved their IPR policies. Among the PSUs, Indian Oil Corporation and Bharat Heavy Electricals Ltd. are worth mentioning. Among private industries, there are many industries, which have started their own IPR cells and it may not be possible to list all of them here. There is no doubt that private industries have responded very well to the new IPR regime in terms of filing patent applications.

First Policy Breakthrough

Ministry of Science and Technology issued the guidelines "Instructions for Technology Transfer and Intellectual Property Rights" in March 2000, which would help in enhancing the motivation of scientists, research Institutions and universities in projects funded by the Department of Science and Technology, Department of Biotechnology, Department of Scientific and Industrial Research and Department of Ocean Development. The salient features of the guidelines are:

1. Institutions shall be encouraged to seek protection of intellectual property rights in respect of the results of R&D. They may retain the ownership of such IPR. Here 'Institutions' mean any technical, scientific or academic establishment, where research is carried out through funding by the central and/or the state governments.
2. The Institutions shall take necessary steps to commercially exploit patents on exclusive or on non-exclusive basis.
3. The owner institution is permitted to retain the benefits and earnings generated out of the IPR. The institution may determine the share of inventor(s) and other persons from such actual earnings. However, such share shall be limited to one third of the actual earnings.
4. IPR generated through joint research by institution(s) and industrial concern(s) through joint efforts can be owned jointly by them or as may be mutually agreed to by them through a written agreement. The institution and industrial concern may transfer the technology to a third party for commercialisation on exclusive/non-exclusive basis. The third party, exclusively licensed to market the innovation in India, must manufacture the product in India. The joint owners may share the benefits and earnings arising out of commercial exploitation of the IPR.

5. The owner institution shall set apart not less than 25% of the revenue generated from IPR to create a Patent Facilitating Fund which shall be utilized by the institution for updating inventions, filing new patent applications and protecting IP rights against infringement, and for building competency in the area of IPR and related issues.
6. The Government shall have a royalty free license for the use of the Intellectual property for the purposes of the Government of India.

This is a major departure in the approach and policy towards managing inventions in India by the Ministry of Science and Technology. In order to have a uniform policy of the government in this respect, it may be useful to have a suitable law in this regard. It is obvious that with more and more autonomy to research institutions in regard to IPR and technology transfer, these institutions, and the scientists working there, would have stronger motivation to invent products and processes, which are required by the market.

Innovations Related Incentives

An innovative industry in India can gain competitive advantage in the market if it develops the necessary expertise and skills in developing and manufacturing new products, which are patented. For example, the advantage of a three year excise duty exemption or exemption from Drugs Price Control Order may translate into reserves/ income which may offset the cost towards R&D. In order to promote R&D and innovation in Indian industries, Government of India provides a number of fiscal incentives and support measures to industries. With increasing public private partnership in technology development through schemes of Technology Development Board, Drug and Pharmaceutical Board and NMILTI, the following incentives would be extremely useful in promoting the culture of innovation and intellectual property protection in industries and academic and R&D institutions.

Excise Duty Waiver on Patented Products

All goods falling under the Schedule to the Central Excise Tariff 1985 are exempt from the excise duty for a period of 3 years from the date of commencement of commercial production provided such goods are manufactured by a wholly owned Indian company and such goods are designed and developed by such Indian company and the goods so designed are patented in any two countries outside India namely, USA, Japan and any country of the European Union. The manufacturer, before commencing commercial production must obtain a certificate from the Department of Scientific and Industrial Research for claiming the benefit.

Exemption from Drug Price Control Order

Bulk drugs produced based on indigenous R&D are exempt from drug price control for a period of 5 years from the date of commencement of commercial production provided that they are produced from the basic stage by a process of manufacture developed by the unit through its own R&D efforts. In case of a drug, which has not been produced elsewhere, if developed and produced indigenously, it would be placed outside the price control order for a period of 10 years from the ate of commencement of commercial production. In order to establish that a process or a product has been developed through indigenous R&D, novelty of the process or product would have to be ensured. In other words a patent would have to be necessarily obtained for claiming the benefit.

Weighted Tax Deduction on R&D Expenditure

Weighted tax deduction @ 150% on R&D expenditure is available to companies engaged in the business of biotechnology, or the business of manufacture or production of drugs, pharmaceuticals, electronic equipment, computers, telecommunication equipment, chemicals and manufacture of aircraft and helicopters. The expenditure on scientific research in relation to drugs and pharmaceuticals shall include expenditure incurred on clinical trials of drugs, obtaining approval from the regulatory authority under any Central, State or provincial Act and the filing of a patent application in India.

Accelerated Depreciation Allowance

Depreciation allowance at a higher rate is available in respect of plant and machinery installed for manufacturing goods based on indigenous technology developed in recognized in-house R&D units, Government R&D institutions, national laboratories and Scientific and Industrial Organizations (SIRO). The present rate of depreciation for plant and machinery is 40% as against 25% for other plants and machinery.

Tax Holiday to R&D Companies

Tax holiday is available to approved companies engaged in scientific and industrial R&D activities on commercial lines for ten consecutive assessment years. This incentive is applicable to any commercial company that has its main objective and activities in the area of scientific and industrial R&D. This would be applicable to companies approved after March 31, 2000 but before April 1, 2003.

Income Tax Relief on R&D Expenditure

Under Section 35(1)(i) of the Income Tax Act 1961, the revenue expenditure on scientific research, by recognized R&D units, on activities related to the business of the company is allowed full deduction. Under Section 35(1)(iv) expenses of a capital nature could be deducted totally from the income of the year in which the expenses have been incurred.

Tax Deduction for Sponsoring Research

Section 35(2AA) of the IT Act 1961 provides for a weighted tax deduction of 125% for expenses on sponsoring research programmes at National laboratories functioning under ICAR, CSIR, ICMR, DRDO, Department of Biotechnology, Department of Atomic Energy, Department of Electronics; IIT and universities.

The Science and Technology Policy 2003[11]

The Science and Technology Policy released in 2003 is upbeat on intellectual property rights and related issues. It focuses a great deal on the transformation of new ideas into commercial successes, which is considered vitally important to the nation's ability to achieve high economic growth and global competitiveness. Accordingly, special emphasis will be given not only to R&D and the technological factors of innovations but also to the other equally important social, institutional and market factors. Value addition and creation of wealth through reassessment, redistribution and repositioning of our intellectual, capital and material resource will be achieved through effective use of science and technology.

The Policy states that IPR has to be viewed, not as a self contained and distinct domain, but rather as an effective policy instrument that would be relevant to wide ranging socio-economic, technological and political concepts. The generation and protection of competitive intellectual property from Indian R&D programmes will be encouraged and promoted. The process of globalization is leading to situations where collective knowledge of societies normally used for common good is converted to a proprietary knowledge for the commercial profit of a few. Action will be taken to protect our indigenous knowledge systems, primarily through national policies, supplemented by supportive international action. For this purpose, IPR systems, which specially protect scientific discoveries and technological innovations arising out of such traditional knowledge will be designed and implemented. Our legislation with regard to patents, copyrights and other forms of intellectual property rights will ensure that maximum incentives are provided for individual inventors, and to our scientific and technological community, to undertake large scale and rapid commercialization, at home and abroad.

The development of skills and competence to manage IPR and to leverage its influence will be given a major thrust. This area calls for significant technological insights and legal expertise and will be handled differently from the present, and with high priority. Efforts will be made to synergy between industry and scientific research by creating Autonomous Technology Transfer Organizations as associate organizations of universities and national laboratories to facilitate the transfer to industry, of the know how generated.

The above action strategy has emerged from the following policy objectives:

- To encourage research and innovation in areas of relevance for the economy and the society, particularly by promoting close and productive interaction between private and public institutions in science and technology;
- To establish an intellectual property rights regime, which maximizes the incentives for the generation and protection of intellectual property by all types of inventors. The regime would also provide a strong, supportive and comprehensive policy environment for speedy and effective domestic commercialization of such inventions so as to be maximal in the public interest and to promote international science and technology cooperation towards achieving the goals of national development and security, and make it a key element of our international relations;

The Policy objectives in regard to intellectual property rights were formulated with the overall perspective that knowledge has become a source of economic might and power. This has led to increased restrictions on sharing of knowledge, to new norms of intellectual property rights, and to global trade and technology control regimes. Scientific and technological developments today also have deep ethical, legal and social implications. There are deep concerns in society about these. The ongoing globalization and the intensely competitive environment have a significant impact on the production and service sectors.

Experience of Indian universities

Until 1995 the culturė of protecting their inventive work through patents by universities and academic institutions was almost nonexistent. Efforts made by multiple agencies in the country have made some difference in the situation, which is obvious from the data and analysis that follow. The Table 5.1 below shows the filings of patent applications by the Indian academic institutions in India.

Table 5.1

Year	*Number of Patent Applications Filed by Academic Institutes Other than IITs and IISc*	*Number of Patent Applications Filed by IITs and IISc*	*Total Number of Patent Applications*
1995	4	31	35
1996	11	18	29
1997	23	15	38
1998	16	34	50
1999	30	32	62
2000	36	42	78
2001	33	63	96
2002	33	46	79

The Table 8.2 shows the growth in filings in two blocks of four years; 1995-1998 and 1999-2002.

Table 8.2

Block period	*Applications Filed During 1995-1998*	*Applications Filed During 1999-2002*	*Percentage Increase in Number of Applications Filed*
Academic institutes other than IITs and IISc	54	132	244
IITs and IISc	98	183	187
Total	**152**	**315**	**207**

It may be noted that out of 132 patent applications filed during 1999-2002 by institutions other than IITs and IISc, 53 applications (40% of the applications) were filed with full technical, legal and financial support of the PFC of TIFAC.

Epilogue

A statement of purpose (SOP) is always helpful in fixing targets and goals because fulfilment of a purpose is satisfying. We have to have an SOP to develop a pool of well informed and trained human resource, deploy sufficient facilities (hardware and software) and, create and promote an enabling environment for generating, protecting and managing intellectual property for progress of science, technology and arts leading to growth of trade and industry and well being of the society. People say that Rome was not built in a day. Any physical process, including development, has to absorb some finite time before taking a shape. We have made a good start by rising to the occasion and putting in place some very useful systems and policies. It is the beginning and we have to go a long way!

REFERENCES

1. The Patents Act, 1970 as amended by Patents (Amendment) Act 2005, Commercial Law Publisher (India) Private Ltd., 2005.
2. The Protection of Plant Varieties and Farmers' Rights Act, 2001 along with Protection of Plant Varieties and Farmers' Rights Rules 2003; Akalank Publications, New Delhi; 2003.
3. The Copyright Act 1957 as amended up to 1999 along with Copyright Rules 1958 and International Copyright Order 1999; 2005.
4. The Design Act 2000 along with Design Rules 2001; Universal Law Publishing Co. Ltd., New Delhi; 2004.
5. The Trademarks Act 1999 along with trade Marks Rules 2002; Commercial Law Publisher (India) Private Ltd., 2004.
6. The Geographical Indications of Goods (Registration and Protection) Act, 1999 along with Geographical Indications of Goods (Registration and Protection) Rules 2002; Universal Law Publishing Co. Ltd., New Delhi; 2004.
7. The Semiconductor Integrated Circuits Layout Design Act 2000 along with Semiconductor Integrated Circuits Layout Design Rules 2001; Universal Law Publishing Co. Ltd., New Delhi; 2005.
8. R&D Statistics Department of Science and Technology, Government of India, May, 2002.
9. Instructions for Technology Transfer and Intellectual Property Rights, Department of Science and Technology, March 2000.
10. Research and Development in Industry: An Overview; Department of Scientific and Industrial Research, Government of India, 2002.
11. Science and Technology Policy 2003, Department of Science and Technology
12. IPR Bulletin, Vol.5, No 8, August 1999; Technology Information, Forecasting and Assessment Council.
13. IPR Bulletin, Vol. 9, No. 10, October 2003; Technology Information, Forecasting and Assessment Council.

(The views expressed above are those of the author and not of the organizations he is affiliated to)

7

Kyrghyz Patent, State Agency on Science and Intellectual Property in Kyrghyzstan

Kyrgyz State Agency on Science and Intellectual Property

(Based on the scientific material provided by the Kyrgyz State Agency on Science and Intellectual Property received through the Embassy of India in Bishkek, Kyrgyzstan)

A Department of Intellectual Property of Kyrghyzstan was established by the Government of the Kirghiz Republic on June 15, 1993 under the State Committee on Science and New Technologies as an organization to manage the patents. It has been a nucleus of patent system and system of intellectual property within the country. These 10 years witnessed the development of the integral and harmonious system of intellectual property in the country including legislative, structural and functional components. The State Agency of Intellectual Property was formed in March 1996 within the Government of the Kirghiz Republic, which has been transformed through a decree of the President of the Kirghiz Republic dated 28.12.2000 into the State Agency on Science and Intellectual Property in the Government of Kirghiz Republic – KyrghyzPatent – with the purpose of further development of scientific potential in connection with transfer to the Agency of the functions of the department within the State Committee on Science and New Technologies, and also with the transfer and transformation of the Kirghiz Scientific Research Institute of the Scientific and Technical Information to the Center of the Scientific and Technical Informatio.,

Presently KyrghyzPatent is the state body carrying out a uniform state policy in the field of science, technics and new technologies, innovations, protection of the rights on objects of the industrial property, copyright and adjacent rights, and also nonconventional objects of intellectual property (Figure 7.1). Special attention in the functioning of KyrghyzPatent is given to legislative maintenance of regulation of attitudes in the field of intellectual property. Corresponding legal norms and basis have been introduced during its functioning in the form of various positions and laws determining the mechanisms of legal aspects on concrete objects of intellectual property.

In the field of international cooperation KyrghyzPatent conducts close cooperation with the World Organization of Intellectual Property (subsequently referred to as WIPO). Within the framework of the concluded Intergovernmental and Interdepartmental agreements KyrghyzPatent continues to develop active cooperation with various International organizations, such as European Patent Department (EPO), Euroasian Patent Organization (EAPO), and also with other foreign patent departments of the countries of the CIS.

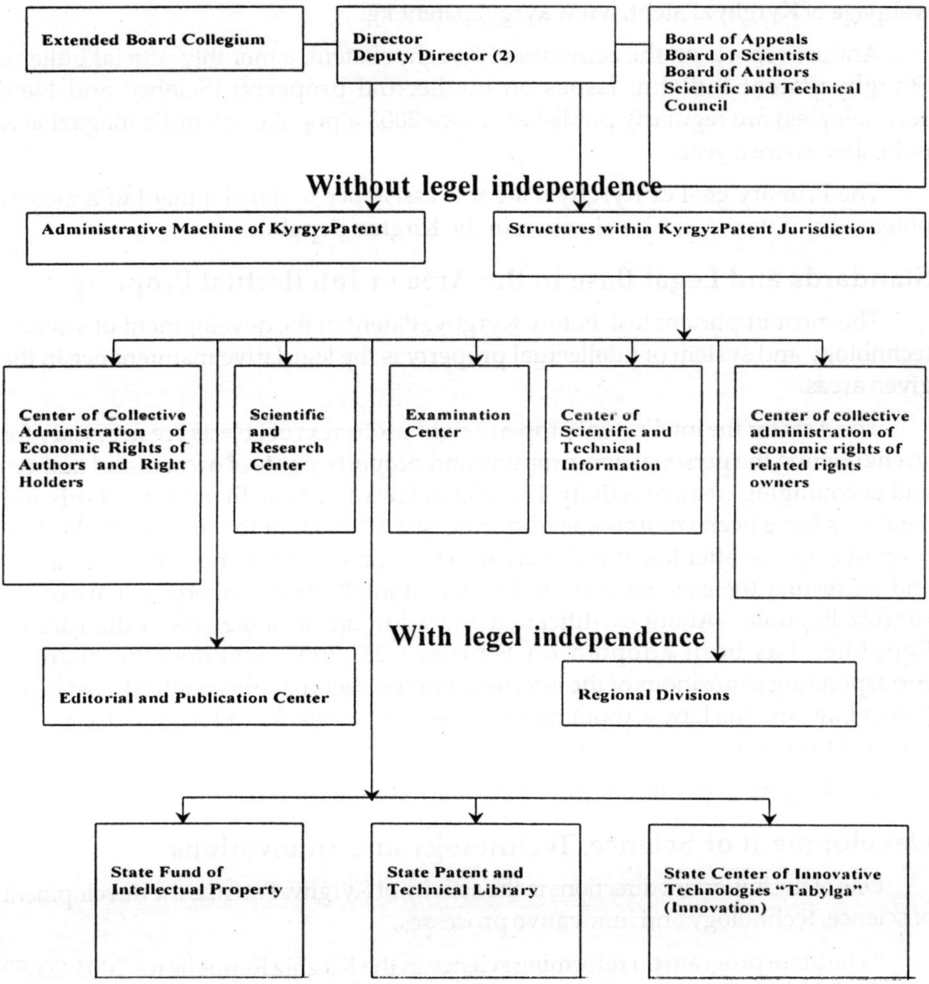

Figure 7.1: Kyrgyz Patent Framework

The significant attention is given to the development of a system of examination of the industrial property. In relation to the market conditions, the big work is carried out by KyrghyzPatent on regulatory mechanisms in the field of the copyright and the adjacent rights. One of the directions of its activity is the state registration of objects of the copyright and the adjacent rights, and also performance of functions of the organization of collective management by property rights of authors and legal owners.

Currently the scientific potential of the Republic that is under the supervision of KyrghyzPatent, is concentrated in more than 50 scientific research institutes, national centers, academies and universities, where systems work on the development of science and technology is carried out.

One of the key tasks of the KyrghyzPatent is the supply of the information on the processes of creation, rights protection and use of objects of intellectual property. A plenty of patent information has been colleted which is available on Internet on the webpage of KyrghyzPatent, www.kyrgyzpatent.kg.

Annual reports on the activities of KyrghyzPatent, a monthly official bulletin (KyrghyzPatent Bulletin: Issues on intellectual property) (Science and New Technologies) are regularly published. Since 2003 a popular scientific magazine is published twice a year.

The Primary goal of KyrghyzPatent is assistance to development of a mental potential and its practical realization in the Kirghiz Republic.

Standards and Legal Base in the Area of Intellectual Property

The most important task before KyrghyzPatent in the development of science, technology and system of intellectual property is the legislative maintenance in the given areas.

The Acts for the intellectual property right protection of objects are necessary for strengthening the personal non-property and property rights of owners and authors and encouraging creative activity. 12 national laws and more than 30 standards and legal acts have been commissioned during last 10 years in the area of intellectual property. Special attention is given on the development of new normative legal acts and perfecting the existing ones in the area of intellectual property. A Law of the Kirghiz Republic «About modification and additions in some acts of the Kirghiz Republic» has been adopted on February 27, 2003, wherein the changes corresponding to positions of the international contracts have been introduced in the Patent Law and the Law «About trade marks, service marks and names of places of origin of the goods».

The Kirghiz Republic has joined 20 international contracts.

Development of Science, Technology and Innovations

One of the important directions in the activity of KyrghyzPatent is the development of science, technology and innovative processes.

"The State program on reforming science in the Kirghiz Republic for 2003-2005" No.144 dated 19.03.2003 has been developed and realized, and also there is the Law

Laws of the Kirghiz Republic in the Area of Intellectual Property

No.	Nomenclature of Legal Act	Date of Entering into Force
1.	The civil code, Part 2, section 5 "Intellectual property"	01.03.1998
2.	Patent law	04.02.1998
3.	About trade marks, service marks and names of places of the origin of the goods	28.02.1998
4.	About the copyright and the adjacent rights	23.02.1998
5.	About the legal protection of computer programs and databases	04.04.1998
6.	About the legal protection of topology of integrated microcircuits	10.04.1998
7.	About commercial secret	10.04.1998
8.	About the legal protection of selection achievements	26.06.1998
9.	About restriction of monopoly activity, development and protection of competition	15.04.1994
10.	About the service inventions, useful models, industrial samples	13.08.1999
11.	About company names	31.12.1999
12.	About patent attorneys	28.02.2001

International Agreements Administered by WIPO, WTO, UPOV

No.	Name of Agreement	Date of Joining
1.	Convention establishing the WIPO	25.12.1991
2.	Paris Convention for the Protection of Industrial Property	25.12.1991
3.	Madrid Agreement concerning International Registration of Trade Marks	25.12.1991
4.	Patent Cooperation Treaty (!")	25.12.1991
5.	Euroasian Patent Convention	13.01.1996
6.	Nice Agreement on the International Classification of Goods and Services for Registration of Marks	10.12.1998
7.	Locarno Agreement establishing the International Classification of Industrial Samples	10.04.1998
8.	Vienna Agreement establishing the International Classification of the Figurative Elements of Marks	26.06.1998

9.	Marakkesh Agreement establishing the World trading organization (WTO), the appendix 1!: Agreement on Trade-Related Aspects of Intellectual Property Rights (TRIPS Agreement)	20.12.1998
10.	Strasbourg Agreement on International Patent Classification (IPC)	10.09.1999
11.	WIPO Copyright Treaty	10.12.1998
12.	Bern Agreement for the Protection of Literary and Artistic Work	08.07.1999
13.	International Convention for the Protection of New Varieties of Plants (UPOV)	26.06.2000
14.	Patent Law Treaty (PLT)	26.11.2001
15.	Geneva Phonogram Convention (on protection of manufacturers' interests from illegal reproduction of their soundtracks)	12.10.2002
16.	WIPO Performances and Phonograms Treaty	15.08.2002
17.	Trademark Law Treaty (TLT)	15.08.2002
18.	Hague Agreement On Industrial Samples International Deposition	17.03.2003
19.	Budapest Treaty on International Recognition of the Deposit of Microorganisms for the Purposes of Patent Procedure	17.05.2003
20.	International Convention for the Protection of Performers, Producers of Phonograms (the Roman convention)	17.05.2003

"About science and about bases of the state scientific and technical policy" No.1485-XII dated 15.04.1994.

Development of innovative processes is the major problem of today. Significant work on development of innovative activity in Kirghiz Republic is carried out with the Center of Innovative Technologies "Innovation" of KyrghyzPatent at which the innovative fund of the Kirghiz Republic has been created. In accordance with the Decree "About measures on further development of industry and innovative activity in the Kirghiz Republic" No. 26 dated 19.01.2001 of the President of the Kirghiz Republic a Council has been established on development of industry and innovative activity under the President of the Kirghiz Republic, and the functions of Secretary have been assigned to KyrghyzPatent.

KyrghyzPatent has worked out a Concept of the state innovative policy of the Kirghiz Republic for 2003-2005. The purpose of the given Concept is the creation of conditions for steady economic growth, an output of innovative production on the internal and external markets due to increase in technological level and competitiveness of manufacture. The mechanisms of realization of the state innovative policy have been submitted in the Concept. Finance-credit, legislative and normative-legal mechanisms, institutional transformations, and mechanisms in the sphere of education, export and customs regulation have been listed out among these mechanisms

A business project on "Electronic-commercial system - Innovative scientific and technical potential of the Kirghiz Republic" has been developed.

"A Catalogue of Innovative Resources of Kirghiz Republic in the field of Science and Technology" has been prepared with commercial proposals of authors on the basis of the completed research and developmental works in 1999-2001. The catalogue includes 288 scientific works.

System of the Scientific and Technical Information of the Kirghiz Republic

The current most actual problem faced by the country is the creation of necessary conditions and favorable environment for the development of science and wider application of its products in the economy of Kyrghyzstan on the basis of applying the achievements of science and technology. Development of complex measures on interaction of science and production, *i.e.* creation of an infrastructure of transfer of the scientific and technical information (hereinafter, STI) in practical application of information resources in the area of STI. A first step in resolving these problems has been the adoption of the Law of the Kirghiz Republic "About System of the Scientific and Technical Information" No. 108 dated 08.10.1999. Similarly additional changes are at present being made in this law for improvement of functioning of the scientific and technical information system.

The national STI system was based on scientific research institute (NTI) till 2001, which got further transformed into the Center of Scientific and Technical Information (CNTI) at KyrghyzPatent by the Governmental Order No. 100 of 15.03.01.

The primary goals of CNTI are:

- Participation in the development and realization of the state policy and the state programs in the sphere of the scientific and technical information;
- Collection, processing, storage and distribution of the scientific and technical information;
- Participation in the creation and development of the national system of the scientific, technical and economic information, in the formation of information resources of nation-wide value;
- Formation of the state information resources and STI systems on the basis of domestic and foreign sources;
- Providing help and analytical information in sphere of the scientific, technical and economic information to the interested state organizations, legal and physical persons;
- Organization and coordination of the international cooperation and exchange of the scientific and technical information within the framework

of the competence according to the international contracts of the Kirghiz Republic.

CNTI carries out the following functions in pursuance of the assigned tasks:

- Gives the information on condition and development of science, techniques and technologies;
- Regularly carries out collection, processing and analysis of domestic and foreign sources of STI;
- Organizes and coordinates activity of system of scientific and technical establishments;
- Carries out researches according to the requirement and to forecast the tendencies of the development of STI, formations and rational use of national and state information resources;
- Participates in preparation of projects of normative legal certificates and programs of development in the sphere of STI, necessary standards and qualifiers in the field of scientific and technical information products and services;
- Carries out the state registration of the research and developmental works, protected candidate and thesis for a doctor's degree;
- Issues information reports and distributes information leaflets about scientific and technical achievements and the advanced know-how in the Kirghiz Republics;
- Gathers data on scientific editions, collections of proceedings, about carrying out of scientific conferences, seminars and meetings, industrial, agricultural and trading exhibitions and fairs;
- Carries out other activity which corresponds to the aims and issues of CITI and not contradicting the legislation of the Kirghiz Republic.

The prospects of the development of STI consist in expansion of the field of activity of STI, in particular: development of the international cooperation and transfer of technologies for information interchange by joining the international database and creation of a national database on scientific and technical achievements (reference document), in which in future the most oustanding research and developmental works will enter (the data on inventions, useful models, industrial samples), registered in Kyrghyzstan. This would provide entry to the information space of the countries of the Commonwealth of Independent States (CIS) for exchange of data on scientific and technical achievements and readily available access to the desired information by the scientists of the Republic.

8

Development of the Intellectual Property Protection System in Lebanon

Souheir Nadde

(Legal Trade Coordinator, Ministry of Economic and Trade, Lebanon)

INTRODUCTION

Ever since the 1920's, Lebanon was keen to promote intellectual creativity and to confirm the importance of human creativity in the evolution of societies and cultures. Accordingly, the rights of intellectuals including their innovations and creations in literature, arts, sciences and industry, were highly protected via a law passed in 1924 and the signature of numerous international treaties on intellectual property rights. The law, which aimed to protect and regulate the Commercial, Industrial, Literary, Artistic and Musical Property[1] [[1]Resolution No. 2385 dated January 1 S\ 1924, concerning the "Regu1ations and Systems of Commercial, Industrial, Literary, Artistic and Musical Property (hereinafter "the 1924 Law")] is considered among the oldest in the Middle East region and the Arab World.

On the international arena, the emergence of the World Trade Organization (WTO) sited Intellectual Property (IP) at the core of international trade regulation, and made it the subject of international trade rules. Therefore, countries were solicited to participate in the multi-lateral trade system and to adopt an "international" model of intellectual property protection. The request for full compliance with the TRIPs Agreement has left these countries in a state of hurry to update their IP laws and provide the necessary legal and enforcement framework to apply them.

For this purpose, Lebanon enacted new and modern laws on the protection of Copyright (in 1999) and Patents (in 2000) and is currently developing a new legislation on Trademarks and Geographical Indications. Moreover, Lebanon signed a Free Trade Agreement (FTA) with the European Community (the ED Association Agreement) which requires Lebanon to ensure protection in conformity with international standards including adhering to new IP conventions.

POLICY FORMULATION AND IMPLEMENTATION

Administrative Structure

The Intellectual Property Protection Office (IPPO) at the Ministry of Economy and Trade (MOET) is the national body responsible for administering and enforcing intellectual property in Lebanon. It is also responsible for fostering the use of intellectual property systems and encouraging invention, innovation and creativity. The main activities of the IPPO are the following:

- Registering intellectual property rights (Patents, copyrights, trademarks, industrial designs, etc.) as well as any resulting legal act (transfer of rights, licensing, etc.);
- Enforcing intellectual property rights *ex-officio* or at the request of right holders to stop any act of IPR piracy;
- Participating in the drafting of new IP laws and regulations;
- Raising public awareness among the public and private sectors including conducting trainings and organizing seminars.

Laws and Regulations

The protection of intellectual property is ensured in Lebanon via the following specific legislation:

- Resolution No.2385/1924 issued on January 17, 1924, amended by the law of 31/1/1946, concerning the "Regulations and Systems of Commercial, Industrial, Literary, Artistic and Musical Property in Lebanon";
- Law No. 75/99 issued on April 13, 1999 concerning the Protection of Literary and Artistic Property (the Copyright Law); and Decision No. 16/2002 concerning the implementation of Article 25 of the Copyright Law.
- Law No. 240 issued on August 7, 2000, concerning Patents and including Protection for Plant Variety, Layout Designs of Integrated Circuits, and Undisclosed Information (the Patent Law);

Additional provisions related to enforcing or administering intellectual property are found under the following legislation: Customs Law, Criminal Law, Law on Civil Procedures, Law instituting the Council of State, Law on Obligations and Contracts, Law on Judicial Fees, Law on the Establishment of the Central Inspection, Law on General Accountancy, Law on Civil Servants, Law related to the Production Manufacture, Sale and Import of Wine, Law on Fraud Control, Law on Alcohols and Drugs, etc.

Copyright

A new and modern Copyright Law was enacted on April 3, 1999, and entered into force on June 6, 1999. The copyright protection originally available to literary and artistic works is now extended to computer software, video films and all kind of audio-visual works. The law now provides stiffer penalties for offenders and better compensation to the persons whose rights have been infringed. The manner in which the copyright is breached has also been extended.

It is to be noted that Article 25 of the Law spells out an exception related to computer programs, allowing the making of copies for educational purposes. Such an exception cannot apply unless an implementing decision, determining the copying mechanism, the categories of computer programs that may be copied and the number of copies allowed, is issued by the concerned ministers. A new decision No. 16/2002 has been passed on July 1 st, 2002 and takes into consideration the limits of fair use as provided by both Article 9(2) of the Berne Convention and Article 13 of the TRIPS Agreement.

Patents

A new, modern and TRIPS compatible Patent Law was enacted on August 7,2000, and entered into force on August 14, 2000. The Law provides a patent protection for inventions and plant varieties and a *sui generis* protection for layout designs of integrated circuits. Furthermore, the law provides protection for undisclosed information. According to an assessment conducted by the World Intellectual Property Organization (WIPO) on July 2002, the Patent Law is in complete conformity with the TRIPS Agreement. It was also pointed out that the provisions of the Plant Varieties exceed the minimum requirements of the TRIPS Agreement.

Plant Varieties

Plant varieties are provided protection by patents in accordance with TRIPS Article 27(3)(b). They are defined in accordance with the provisions of the International Convention for the Protection of New Varieties of Plants and in compliance with the TRIPS Agreement.

Topographies of Integrated Circuits

Integrated Circuits are provided *sui generis* protection under Section III of the Patent law. The related provisions which were inspired, to a large extent, from the Intellectual Property French Code are in compliance with the requirements of the TRIPS Agreement.

Undisclosed Information

The Trade/commercial secrets are provided protection under Article 579 of the Criminal law. In addition, Article 47 of the Patent Law provides protection for undisclosed information as required by TRIPS Article 39. Enforcement procedures and adequate remedies are available in such a way to permit effective action against any act of infringement of undisclosed information including 2 months to 3 years imprisonment and/or a fine of 5 to 50 million Lebanese Liras.

Trademarks and Geographical Indications

Trademarks are provided protection under the "Regulations and Systems of Commercial, Industrial, Literary, Artistic and Musical Property in Lebanon" (the 1924 law). The provisions of the 1924 law along with the Paris Convention and the Madrid Agreement cover the obligations of the TRIPS Agreement. This law also provides protection to service marks, trade names and three-dimensional trademarks. The 1924 Law does not explicitly protect notorious trademarks and geographical indications. However, those are provided protection via Lebanon's membership to the Paris Convention and the Madrid Agreement respectively. Moreover, Geographical indications are provided protection under the provisions of the new Law on Customs, the Law on Fraud Control and the Criminal Law.

In addition, MOET is developing a new and modem legislation on Trademarks and Geographical Indications which will take into consideration the industrial developments since 1924 (date of the related law now in force) and the requirements of the TRIPS Agreements concerning the protection of well-known marks and geographical indications.

Industrial Designs

Industrial designs are provided protection under Articles 48-67 and Articles 111-136 of the 1924 Law. The above-mentioned Articles meet the obligations of the TRIPS Agreement, as well as the related provisions of the Paris Convention.

MOET is revising the provisions of the 1924 law related to Industrial Designs in order to modernize the legislation in this regard.

Unfair Competition

Unfair Competition is provided protection under Articles 97 and 98 of the 1924 Law.

Enforcement of Intellectual Property

It is important to highlight that the implementation of the Intellectual Property legislation (in particular the 1999 Copyright Law) remains a significant challenge for Lebanon especially that the Lebanese Intellectual Property Protection Office (IPPO) lacks specialized staff, proper equipment, computerized and specialized network and related enforcement capacities in order to implement effectively the obligations of the Law.

Despite the limited human and technical capabilities of enforcement present within the Lebanese Government today, the relevant bodies are taking effective action at the request of the right holder to stop any act of IPR piracy that might infringe on their rights. In this regard, MOET has conducted raids following all the requests it received from right holders in which heavy fines and prison sentences were pronounced against the violators by the Judiciary. Moreover, since the second half of 2002, IPPO and Customs have been cooperating together on combating intellectual property piracy by taking actions *exofficio*, in particular interdicting and seizing pirate products entering the country and confiscating infringed goods wherever they are found on borders or in the country. Furthermore, joint working groups incorporating inspectors from IIPO, the Consumer Protection Office, the VAT department and the Customs have been established to investigate the various violations in relevant fields including IPR violations.

Furthermore, the Ministry of Economy and Trade, in coordination with different parties (WIPO, USAID, IFPI, l'Union des Fabricants, BSA, Microsoft and others), has been launching public awareness campaigns, along with training and seminars aimed at educating the relevant bodies to the role and impact of Intellectual Property Rights and improving their skills in their respective fields. The public awareness campaigns include video clips on IPR awareness, distribution of awards, production of posters and flyers on software piracy etc.).

In addition, the Lebanese Government has signed an Enterprise Licensing and Premier Services Agreement with the Microsoft Corporation to gain access to the most advanced software and computer programs needed in the training of public sector employees. The Agreement provides the Government immediate access to the most advanced versions of the enterprise products with 24X7 support and proactive operational reviews, and train the-trainer programs to develop skills of public sector employees. This significant step clearly shows the Lebanese Government's efforts to enforce IPRS and eliminate existing piracy starting with its Public Institutions.

MEMBERSHIP OF INTERNATIONAL INTELLECTUAL PROPERTY CONVENTIONS AND REGIONAL OR BILATERAL AGREEMENTS

Lebanon is a member of the following conventions:

- Convention establishing the World Intellectual Property Organization (in 1986);/Paris Convention for the Protection of Industrial Property (in 1924 and ratified the London Act in 1947);
- Berne Convention for the Protection of Literary and Artistic Works (Rome Act in 1947);
- Madrid Agreement for the Repression of False Indications of Source on Goods (in 1924 and ratified the London Act in 1947);
- Nice Agreement Concerning the International Classification of Goods and Services for the Purposes of the Registration of Marks (Nice Act in 1961);
- International convention for the protection of Performers, Producers of phonograms and Broadcasting organizations (in 1997);
- Universal Copyright Convention (in 1959).

In addition, Lebanon has committed itself under the EU Association Agreement to ratify the last versions of IP conventions to which Lebanon is already member and to adhere to new Conventions on IP (5 years after the entry into force of the Association Agreement). Accordingly, Lebanon shall adhere to the following conventions by March 2008:

- The Stockholm Act of the Paris Convention for the protection of industrial property;

- The Paris Act of the Berne Convention for the Protection of Literary and Artistic Works;
- The Geneva Act of the Nice Agreement concerning the International Classification of Goods and Services for the purposes of the Registration of Marks;
- The Patent Cooperation Treaty (Washington, 1970, amended in 1979 and modified in 1984);
- The Budapest Treaty on the International Recognition of the deposit of Microorganisms for the Purposes of Patent Procedure;
- The Protocol to the Madrid Agreement concerning the international registration of marks;
- The Trademark Law Treaty;
- The International Convention for the Protection of New Varieties of Plants (UPOV);
- The Agreement on Trade-related Aspects of Intellectual Property Rights (The TRIPs Agreement).

The Lebanese Parliament ratified the Patent Cooperation Treaty on June 2002. Lebanon will deposit the instrument of ratification at WIPO in the near future.

EXISTING PROBLEMS

Lebanon currently faces the following problems that need to be addressed:

- Limited human and technical capabilities of enforcement;
- Lack of specialized staff in the IPPO;
- Lack of computerized and specialized network among relevant bodies;
- Lack of specialized judges in courts.

UP COMING ACTIONS AND FUTURE PROSPECT

In recognition of the importance of intellectual property as a "power tool" for economic development and wealth creation, and in order to provide efficient protection for IPR holders, the Lebanese government, specifically the Ministry of Economy and Trade (MOET) is pursuing this issue more actively. Traditionally there has been little awareness and modest communication material developed on IPR. However, recently, MOET in coordination with different parties has been launching public awareness campaigns along with training seminars. To strengthen such efforts, MOET is planning on launching a campaign called "IP Week" that will target companies and consumers. The ultimate aim of the campaign is to increase awareness of IPR and decrease the levels of violations that currently take place.

CONCLUSION

Lebanon is addressing the existing problems by relying on the technical assistance provided by international organizations and some developed countries (France for instance). It is also relying on implementing and enforcing effectively existent agreements on intellectual property rights in order to insure the best and most exhaustive protection.

However, more efforts are still needed to face the challenges encountered in this field. More capacity building is also needed for the staffs of the IPPO and the enforcement bodies to ensure an efficient IP protection in the face of up-coming technologies.

Furthermore, Lebanon should benefit from all the provisions of international agreements to accomplish socio-economic objectives, namely, the freedom to use trans-border technology flows as enshrined in the TRIPS Agreement.

9

THE STATUS OF INTELLECTUAL PROPERTY RIGHTS (IPRs) AND TRIPS AND RELATED PROBLEMS FOR MALAWI

Frade K. Nyondo

(Principal Scientific Officer, National Research Council of Malawi, Lilongwe WE 3, Malawi)

INTRODUCTION

Malawi has laws on Intellectual Property Rights (IPRs) which are aimed at protecting the rights of individuals on their inventions and innovations. Some of the intellectual property legislations existing are the Patents Act 1958, the Trade Marks Act 1958, the Registered Designs Act 1958, and the Trade Description Act 1987. The Patents Act of 1958 provides for a nationally independent system of patent protection with no fields of technology excluded. Under the Patents Act, protection is granted on the first to file principle for a period of 16 years with a possibility for extension and renewal fees are payable from the fourth year.

Malawi has been mindful of the fact that it requires protection of its industrial property in other countries. Because of that it has signed, ratified or acceded to a number of international and regional treaties and conventions such as the Patent Cooperation Treaty, Strasbourg Agreement on International Patent Classification, Lusaka Agreement Establishing the African Regional Industrial Property Organization (ARIPO), the Harare Protocol on Patents and Industrial Designs, and the Banjul Protocol on Marks.

Malawi is a member of the World Trade Organization (WTO) hence bound by the TRIPS Agreement which it is supposed to implement by the year 2006. Under the national law biological materials and biotechnological processes are not patentable which poses some conflicts with the current negotiations to review the TRIPS Agreement. TRIPS form a very important part of the world trade and the main aspect at stake for Malawi is trade in biological materials, especially agricultural products.

LOCATION, SIZE, AND BIODIVERSITY OF MALAWI

Malawi is in South-eastern Africa. It shares borders with Tanzania, Zambia, and Mozambique. The borders between Malawi and the three countries are roads, rivers and lake Malawi. The roads, rivers and the lake are not properly manned by law enforcement agents leading to a lot of informal trade in biological materials. Malawi's total area is 11.8 million ha of which 9.4 million ha is land and the remaining being water.

Malawi is endowed with diverse flora, fauna and micro biota. At least 3,500, 4,000 and 1,000 species of plants, animals and micro-organisms respectively, have been described so far. Fish resources consist between 500 and 1000 species. Almost all the fish species are endemic to Malawi.

BREEDING RESEARCH AND INTELLECTUAL PROPERTY RIGHTS

Various institutions are involved in research in agricultural and biological materials. Some of the public institutions are Department of Agricultural Research and Technical Services (DARTS), University of Malawi, Forestry Research Institute of Malawi (FRIM), and Monkey bay Fisheries Research Unit. The private research institutions are Agricultural Research and Extension Trust (ARET) for tobacco and the Tea Research Foundation of Central Africa (TRF) for tea. In addition, several international organizations fund and are involved in collaborative research in Malawi. Some of these organizations are CIMMYT, IITA/SARRNET, ICRISAT, IRRI, CIP, ICRAF, CIAT and SPGRC. These international institutions have brought in a lot of germplasm for maize, cassava, sweet potatoes, groundnuts, pigeon peas, yams, irish potatoes, agroforestry trees, rice, cowpeas, and beans.

In Malawi, while research is being carried out on the world's major food and industrial crops, breeding work is limited. Most of the research which is carried out is in the field of agronomy, plant protection (pathology and entomology), processing and nutrition, storage, conservation and breeding (for some crop species). Plant breeding is quite limited in that much of the work is on adaptation/performance evaluation on local landraces and materials introduced from CGIAR centres. Some breeding work is being done on crops like maize, rice, tobacco, cotton, coffee and cassava which involves crosses made on local germplasm and crosses made using local and introduced materials. Introduced materials used in breeding are mainly chosen for yield potential and local materials for their adaptability and consumer acceptability. Breeding and evaluation in public research institutions is done on a number of crops. The private seed companies tend to be selective and target their work on crops where hybrid seed is produced because farmers cannot recycle the seed hence a higher turnover for the companies.

Malawi is in the process of developing regulations on Plant Breeders' Rights. A draft document was produced which awaits final refining prior to implementation. However, private seed companies multiplying varieties bred by public research institutions pay a minimal royalty based on hectarage under production. Application of patent laws on biological materials is not in use in Malawi.

BIOTECHNOLOGY RESEARCH

Malawi is not currently involved in basic research of developing biotechnology but is applying technologies developed elsewhere. Several instances exist where research is being done to adapt the various technologies for application. Application of biotechnology is done through tissue culture, vaccine and disease diagnosis, fermentation in dairy and brewery products, production of fuel and DNA analysis.

Tissue Culture

Tissue culture work is done on sweet potato, irish potato (white potato), cassava, yams, bananas, indigenous fruits and agroforestry species. This is done for rapid multiplication of materials and viral disease cleaning. Tissue culture is done at Bvumbwe Agricultural Research Station and Bunda College of Agriculture. Bunda College of Agriculture also participates in tissue culture evaluation of plantlets of cassava and yams from the International Institute for Tropical Agriculture (IIT A).

Fermentation in Dairy and Brewery Products

The Malawi Dairy Industry (MDI) and Dairyboard Malawi produce products like cheese, yoghurt, ice cream and margarine. Microbes used in the production of yoghurt are *Lactobacilus lactis* and *L. bugaricus* (an acid forming and aroma forming bacteria, respectively). *Streptococcus thermophilus* is used in the production of cheese. The Carlsberg Brewery Company uses brewery yeast, *Sacromyces carsbergensis* for fermentation.

Fuel

The Malawi Industrial Research and Technology Development Centre (MIRTDC) is researching on production of biogas by use of naturally occurring microorganisms. The biogas is used in stoves for cooking.

Vaccines and Disease Diagnosis

The Central Veterinary Laboratory is involved in the production of vaccine for East Coast Fever. The laboratory also produces materials (conjugates) used in the diagnostic tests of African Swine Fever. The Ministry of Health under the Expanded Programme on Immunization (EPI) has a country wide administration of vaccines which include BCG, Diphtheria toxoid, Tetanus toxoid and Poliomyelitis. The last three are combined as DTP vaccine.

DNA Analysis

The Bean-Cowpea Research Project at Bunda College of Agriculture has a DNA analysis laboratory. Its main purpose is characterization of beans with respect to their leaf disease reaction.

Currently capacity in the field of biotechnology is very limited. The increasing ways in which the technology can be used call for human resource development in the field. One of the important aspects requiring attention is biosafety. There is need to develop national biosafety regulations and guidelines in order to minimize the dangers emanating from mismanagement of biotechnological applications. The process to formulate such regulations and guidelines is underway.

IMPORTANCE OF TRADE IN AGRICULTURAL PRODUCTS IN THE NATIONAL ECONOMY

Malawi's economy is heavily dependent on agriculture. Agriculture supports 85% of the population and contributes 37% of GDP. Agriculture also contributes 90% to the foreign exchange earnings. Most of the foreign exchange earnings come from crops such as tobacco, tea and coffee (Table 9.1). From the same table, it can be seen that the value of exports in agricultural products has always been over 90% of the total merchandise trade exports and tobacco has contributed over 50%. The contribution of fish, fishery and forestry products to the value of exports has been minimal.

The total trade balance has always been a deficit while that of agricultural products has been a surplus. The value of imports in agricultural products has been rising while the value of exports has been fluctuating. All this has been happening due to Malawi's dependence on a few cash crops such as tobacco, tea and coffee. Malawi as a price taker is very susceptible to prices in the international markets. A fall in the price of tobacco affects the entire economy as it happened in August 1998 when the Kwacha was heavily devalued due to unfavourable prices in the tobacco market.

VALUE OF TRADE IN AGRICULTURE, FISHERY AND FORESTRY PRODUCTS

The value of exports in agricultural products has exceeded the value of imports indicating a surplus balance of trade (Table 9.2). The surplus obtained from the sale of agricultural products has been used to offset some of the deficit incurred in other sectors. It should be noted that most of the agricultural products are sold raw indicating that there is very little value added to them. Lack of transformation of agricultural products into industrial goods means that whatever Malawi trades in cannot be patented.

The agricultural products exported by Malawi in the form of raw materials usually come back as processed products for consumption. Most of the agricultural produce like mangoes get wasted when they are in season. There is need to establish small scale agro-industries for processing such highly perishable agricultural produce. It is pathetic to note that Malawi with a very conducive agricultural

Table 9.1: Trade by Product 1980, 1985, 1990, 1995 in 1000$

	1980		*1985*		*1990*		*1995*	
	Exports	*Imports*	*Exports*	*Imports*	*Exports*	*Imports*	*Exports*	*Imports*
TOTAL Mer Trade	284601	440079	250095	286666	412335	575028	402560	471500
AOR. PROD.	250860	34437	232805	21633	381662	51494	361736	101562
Food and Animal.	95493	23115	110074	13013	91962	410.8	99371	87604
Meat + meat prep		–	–	–	–	--	–	225
Dairy prod + Eggs	6283	3300	6630	4815				
Cereals and prep.	4195	12708	18011	7138	1484	29357	3351	74852
Fruit + Vegetable	3300	936	632	4264	189	2852	2260	
Sugar and Honey	49052	534	5141	239	28339	423	49851	550
Cof+Tea+Coc+Sp.	37891	437	26139	400	577778	341	42897	1119
Feeding Stuffs	1039	21	60704	76	72	261	347	479
Misc. Food	-	1566	76	1023	25	2120	50	3085
Beverage + Tobacco	126679	3314	109643	1671	282528	1049	255564	2851
Beverages	55	1203	4	786	96	1029	176	936
Tobacco	126624	2111	109639	885	282432	20	255388	1915
Crude materials	28162	2401	12952	443	6963	2455	6783	522
Fish + Fish products	2579	4.53	240	336	380	775	215	917
Forest products		27038	-	8218	1993	8058	2043	8057
Agriculture Requisites	391	28176	50	32335		21770	165	82050
Animal vegetable oil	526	5607	136	6506		6902	18	10585

Source: FAO Yearbooks of Trade 1986, 1991 and 1996.

environment imports items such as food from within the countries of the SADC region. However, processing of citrus and indigenous fruits has commenced at a small scale by growers. Currently, training of farmers has started so that they can be canning tomatoes for sale during the period of scarcity.

Table 9.2: Value of Trade in Agricultural Products 1980–1996 in 1000 US$

Year	*Exports*	*Imports*	*Difference*
1980	250860	34437	216423
1981	238276	38114	200162
1982	221406	26229	195177
1983	213933	25455	188477
1984	314196	19781	294415
1985	232805	21633	211172
1986	231638	17373	214265
1987	258215	23824	234391
1988	274018	40056	233962
1989	249198	56733	192465
1990	381662	51494	330168
1991	461593	83341	378257
1992	371236	171350	199886
1993	285967	155635	130332
1994	384149	155503	228646
1995	361736	101562	260174
1996	383418	112677	270741

Source: FAO Yearbooks of Trade 1986, 1991 and 1996.

The value of exports does not include the trade that takes place informally which is substantial but unquantified. There is a lot of crossborder trade between Malawi and its neighbours Zambia, Mozambique and Tanzania and even beyond. It is difficult to account for this because the boundaries are merely rivers, lakes, and roads which are unmanned to a large extent. The value of imports does not account for this informal crossborder trade and the concessionary imports Malawi gets in form of food aid.

The recurrent droughts have forced Malawi to import a lot of food using the scarce foreign exchange and in form of food aid. In 1997, actual maize production was 1,534,462 MT which was lower than the domestic requirements of2,398,600 MT. The domestic requirements indicated in this paper do not include maize for processing into livestock feed and for use in the breweries. The difference had to be offset by food aid and imports.

Malawi is very rich in flora and fauna most of which is not fully exploited when it comes to trade. Table 9.3 shows the value of trade in agricultural, forestry and fishery products from 1980 to 1996. Looking at Tables 11.2 and 11.3, it can be summarized that the contribution of forestry and fishery products to the value of trade has been minimal. In some instances, the surplus from the sale of agricultural products has been used to pay for the imports of the fishery and forestry products. Malawi has concentrated on the sale of fish and timber as other biological products. It has not looked at the other products that are found in the lake that can be exploited. Traditions hinder the exploitation of these other species as Malawians rarely use them for consumption.

Table 9.3: Value of Trade in Agricultural, Fishery and Forestry Products 1980–1996 in 1000 US$

Year	*Exports*	*Imports*	*Difference*
1980	253000	61900	191100
1981	240500	54200	186300
1982	223100	38100	219400
1983	215000	37500	211300
1984	315000	27200	312000
1985	233000	30200	230000
1986	23190	17500	230200
1987	258600	24000	234600
1988	274400	40700	233700
1989	249500	57500	192000
1990	3802000	52300	329700
1991	462000	92000	369600
1992	378100	175800	202300
1993	286200	160900	125300
1994	384400	159600	224800
1995	364000	110500	253500
1996	385700	117550	268150

Source: FAO Yearbooks of Trade 1986, 1991 and 1996.

The range of biological products being traded by Malawi is very narrow. There is need to diversify the biological products it trades in.

In summary, Malawi needs to diversify the range of agricultural and biological products that it trades in. Its vulnerability stems from its dependence on a few agricultural products which arc exported without adding value to them.

SOURCES OF SEED

The bulk of seed used by farmers in Malawi for subsistence production comes from the informal seed sector. For cash crops, most of the seed comes from the formal sector and is improved. The indigenous seed is unimproved and gives low yields but is adapted to those environments and is acceptable to consumers. The low yields obtained from the unimproved seed are, however, a major contribution to the food insecurity at the household and national level. Use of improved seed could substantially improve household and national food security. It is apparent, though, that farmers will continue using unimproved seed and the informal sector will continue being the source of seed for years to come.

Table 9.4 shows the percentages of improved and indigenous seed used in Malawi. It is evident that a large percentage of seed used by farmers for subsistence production is indigenous. For cash crop production, most of the seed is improved.

Table 9.4: Quantities and Types of Seed used

Sl.No.	*Crop*	*Total land Area (ha)*	*Total Quantity Seed Used Tonnes*	*Percent by Seed Types*	
				Improved	*Indigenous*
1.	Maize	1297062	32427	25	75
2.	Groundnuts	140887	12678	1.6	98.4
3.	Beans	148650	11892	8	92
4.	Tobacco	114051	62	95	5
5.	Rice	42189	3164	69	31
6.	Wheat	2483	199	5	95
7.	Pigeon Peas	123088	984	30	70
8.	Soyabeans	40829	–	16	84
9.	Cassava	151941	3404	34	86

Source: Mwendo-Phiri and Chizala, 1999.

Table 9.5 shows the source of seed used for selected crops. It is clear that on-farm saved seed contributes the highest proportion of seed for subsistence production.

Table 9.5: Seed Sources in Percent

Sl.No.	*Crop*	*Formal*		*Informal*	
		Public	*Private*	*Smallholder Commercial*	*On-Farm Saved Seed*
1.	Maize	5	10	10	75
2.	G/nuts	0.2	0.4	1	98.4
3.	Beans	3	1	4	92
4.	Tobacco	0	95	0	5
5.	Rice	69	0	0	31
6.	Wheat	5	0	0	95
7.	Pigeon Peas	6	15	9	70
8.	Soyabeans	4	9	3	84
9.	Cassava	10	24	0	66

Source: Mwendo-Phiri and Chizala, 1999.

The Formal Seed Sector

Malawi has a national seed policy. Emphasis of the policy has been put on variety research and development; pre-basic, basic and certified seed production; and commercial seed production and marketing. There is a Seed Act which was enacted in May, 1988 but is not fully functional because some of the seed regulations are still on draft. However, the Seed Services Unit still plays a major role in ensuring that the quality of seed is satisfactory.

There is a National Seed Committee with membership from various stakeholders both private and public. Its role is to establish a strong and collaborative link between the public and private sectors to ensure efficient planning and implementation of the national seed programmes. Its functions include recommending policies and programmes for the development of the seed industry; promoting training and education in seed technology; and implementing a buffer seed stock programme.

There is a Variety Release Committee which has been in place since late 1970s and is composed of breeders, agronomists, crop protection specialists, socio-economists and user organizations. Its functions are to review the history and performance record of candidate varieties for release, determine their potential contribution, and make recommendations pertaining to their release and entry into the seed multiplication programme.

Malawi has a Quality Control and Certification Agency known as the Seed Services Unit. The unit operates at four research stations of Baka, Lifuwu, Bvumbwe, and Chitedze. Seed quality control is achieved through seed certification schemes (rules and regulations) and seed testing. The Seed Testing Laboratory has been accredited to the International Seed Testing Association (1ST A) since 1971 and follows the Organization of Economic Cooperation and Development seed certification schemes.

Seed multiplication is done by commercial seed companies and individual farmers. The commercial seed companies enter into contracts with commercial farmers. Seed producers are free to use any marketing channels while as before liberalization, the Agricultural Development and Marketing Corporation (ADMARC) was responsible for selling all farm inputs including seed. Donors like the European Union have facilitated the development of the smallholder commercial seed sector. Non-Governmental Organizations (NGOs) also play an important role in providing start up material for farmers to initiate seed multiplication programmes. National Seed Cotton and Milling (NSCM), Pannar Seed Ltd., and ARET are some of the private companies involved in seed multiplication and marketing.

The Informal Seed Sector

About 90% of the national seed requirement is met from the seed saved on-farm from the previous harvest. Dissemination of seed is normally on exchange basis in the informal seed sector. Where the seed is sold, it is less expensive than the seed in the formal seed sector.

Previous Government policies restricted the availability of improved seed of most of the food crops other than maize. The relevant Government policy would therefore be the liberalization of seed production and marketing through the amendment of the Seed Act that would allow smallholder farmers to multiply and trade in all seeds. Liberalization of improved seed neglected by commercial seed companies can now reach farmers at affordable prices.

NGOs such as Action Aid, Christian Service Committee, Concern Universal, Livingstonia Primary Health Care and World Vision International and the donor community such as the EU have initiated seed production projects for smallholder farmers for open pollinated crops such as maize, groundnuts, cowpeas, pigeon peas, soya beans, beans, cassava and sweet potatoes. The seed is produced in groups and farmers give twice the seed they got from these NGOs as payment after harvest. The seed collected is redistributed to other farmers. The seed growers share the seed with their relatives or friends, sell some to the community and keep some for their use.

Another source of seed in the informal sector is recycling and saving seed on farm. To ensure high quality seed, farmers dry it adequately, keep it under cool dry conditions, protect it from pests by smoking and treating with wood ash and storing in rat proof containers.

Some of the sources of varieties in the informal sector include farm saved indigenous varieties which are often mixtures and have been carried over for years; recycled seed of improved varieties; introductions from foreign countries through the formal seed sector; crossborder seed leakage; and importations on food relief programmes.

The informal seed sector plays a very important role for subsistence production. For commercial production, the role of the informal seed sector is minimal. Malawi has liberalized seed production and this brings in the challenge of quality. Smallholder farmers in Malawi use their traditional methods to ensure good quality seed. To increase capacity in seed inspection, the government has licensed some extension workers to do that.

IMPLICATIONS OF THE NEW IPR REGIME UNDER TRIPS

The Convention on Biological Diversity (CBD) provides for unrestricted access to genetic resources, equitable benefit sharing, and sustainable utilization of such resources. Under Section 5 of TRIPS members of WTO are required to provide patent protection for inventions in all fields of technology, whether products or processes, provided that they are new, involve an inventive step and are capable of industrial application. Article 27.3 (b) of Section 5 of TRIPS excludes patentability of plants and animals other than micro-organisms. What does this mean to Malawi?

- Farmers may be alienated from the free use of varieties if breeders are given exclusive rights unless they are informed of the provisions on CBD, International Undertaking on Plant Genetic Resources (IUPGR), TRIPS and Breeders Rights.
- Breeders may not have easy access to germplasm currently being provided by the CGIAR Centres.
- Malawi will need to enforce the protection of its genetic resources

- Malawi will not have easy access to the biotechnologies developed elsewhere
- There will be need to revise the Patent Act of 1958 so that it conforms with the provisions of the TRIPS Agreement
- Malawi will need to commit resources to finalize breeders rights, enforce regulations on access to genetic resources and benefit sharing etc.
- It may be difficult for Malawi to trade in biological products that have been patented by other countries.
- The TRIPS Agreement poses problems regarding who gets the patent the farmer or the researcher

ISSUES TO BE ADDRESSED

- There is an urgent need for public awareness on the CBD provisions, IUPGR, TRIPS and Breeders' Rights
- Revise the Patent Act of 1958 so that it conforms with the provisions of TRIPS. There is a Legal and Patenting Policies Committee under the National Research Council of Malawi (NRCM) which has been dormant due to lack of funds but needs to be rejuvenated so that it revises the Patent Act and other IPRs
- Finalize the Plant Breeders' Rights and consider Animal Breeders' Rights as well
- Develop a national framework law on Access to Genetic Resources and Equitable Benefit Sharing. There is the Genetic Resources and Biotechnology Committee in the NRCM which engaged a consultant to look at this with funding from the World Bank
- Enforce the regulations on Access to Genetic Resources and Benefit Sharing through formulation of Contract Agreement documents
- Finalize the Biotechnology and Biosafety guidelines
- Develop capacity in relevant institutions to undertake some of the above tasks.

To do the above, there will be need for Government and the donor community to provide financial resources.

10

THE STATUS OF INTELLECTUAL PROPERTY RIGHTS IN MALAYSIA

Heng Jee Heng

(Principal Assistant Director, Ministry of Science, Technology and the Environment, Wisma Sime Darby, Jalan Raja Laut, 50662, Kuala Lumpur, Malaysia)

OBJECTIVE

The objective of this country paper is to inform the Conference about the current status of Intellectual Property Rights (IPR) in Malaysia. Besides tracing briefly the advent of IPR legislation in Malaysia, it will also recount the measures undertaken currently by the authorities to ensure the legal framework and enforcement mechanism for IPR in Malaysia are in full harmony with TRIPS by the year 2000. This paper as such, will touch on the salient aspects of the bundle of IPR as protected in Malaysia as well as deliberate on possible implementation issues as the nation moved into the new millenium.

INTRODUCTION

Malaysia has always been on the forefront in respecting and protecting intellectual assets. In fact, it was the growing awareness of IP in Malaysia during the last 20 years that has led her to adopt and to revise many of her national IP legislations. This growing awareness is indeed strikingly visible in the legal profession and those involved in international trade and industry. Also the wonders of Information Technology, office automation and the advancement and modernisation of government services has contributed much to the better IP management system that is now in place in Malaysia.

Prior to independence (1957), Malaysia (Malaya then) adopted legislations from the United Kingdom (UK) with respect to IPR. With independence and the formation of Malaysia in, 1963, these legislations were progressively reviewed and developed to suit local requirements and national growth strategies. The various legislations in force today for all manners of IPR in Malaysia are as shown in Appendix 1.

The history and development of IPR in Malaysia as such, is by no means, unique. Like most developing countries under the British Commonwealth, Malaysia followed closely the form and substance of IPR as practiced in the UK. Even though Malaysia has most of its national legislations in place, strangely enough to this day, registration of industrial designs must still be done in the UK to have its desired effects in Malaysia.

INTELLECTUAL PROPERTY LEGISLATION IN MALAYSIA

To date, the main intellectual properties in Malaysia as protected by law are patents (including petty patents), trademarks and copyrights, industrial designs and confidential information. A brief description of each of these is as follows:

Patents

- Before October 1986, patents were registered in the UK and re-registered in Malaya, Sabah and Sarawak. Malaysia changed from a patent re-registration system to an examination system only in 1986 when the first national legislation on patents, the Patents Act, 1983, which together with the Patents Regulations, 1986, came into force only in 1986.
- However, since a patent registration office was practically non-existent in Malaysia when the Patents Act, 1983 became law, the search and examination functions was performed by proxy via the Standards and Industrial Research Institute of Malaysia (SIRIM).
- To ensure patent protection continues to be current, relevant and valid, the Patents (Amendment Act) 1986 was passed by Parliament in 1986. It was only in October 1990, that patent registration was transferred from SIRIM officially to a newly established dedicated patent registration office, now better known as the Intellectual Property Department (IPD) of the Ministry of Domestic Trade and Consumer Affairs (DOMTRADE). See Appendix 7 for the role of the IPD.
- Currently patents are governed by the Patents (Amendment) Act, 1995 and the regulations made there under.
- The salient aspects of patent protection in Malaysia are as in Appendix 2.

Trade Marks

- Trademark in Malaysia is governed by the Trademark Act of 1976 and the Trademark Regulations, 1983. Both came into force in September 1983.
- As in the case of patents, it is essentially modeled after the United Kingdom Trademarks Act, 1938, In fact, to this day, when processing local trademark applications, British precedents and law continues to be most persuasive.
- The salient aspects of trademark protection in Malaysia are as in Appendix 3.

Industrial Designs

There are 3 pieces of legislations that governs industrial designs in Malaysia. These are:

- The United Kingdom Designs (Protection) Act, 1949 (Peninsular Malaysia)
- The United Kingdom Designs (Protection) Ordinance, Chapter 152 (Sabah)
- The United Kingdom Designs (Protection) Ordinance, Chapter 59 (Sarawak)
- The above 3 Acts provide for the registered proprietor of a design registered under the United Kingdom Registered Design Act, 1949 or any Act amending and substituting for it, to enjoy in the respective parts of Malaysia, "the like privileges and rights as though the Certificate of Registration had been issued with an extension" to these territories. As such, in substance, the law applicable in Malaysia in respect of Registered Designs is the law as applicable in the UK.
- The salient aspects of registered design law in Malaysia are as in Appendix 4.

Copyrights

- The Copyright Act 1987 came into force on December 1987. This Act was amended in 1990. The Copyright (Amendment) Act, 1990 is the only law in Malaysia that governs copyright matters.
- The Copyright Act, 1987 confers exclusive rights to copyright owners to control public performance, reproduction, communication, broadcasting, and distribution of all artistic and literary works.
- The salient aspects of copyright law in Malaysia are as in Appendix 5.

Confidential Information

- The law of confidence in Malaysia is not codified. It is largely based on English Common Law.
- Confidential information covers, *inter alia*, government secrets, trade secrets and artistic secrets
- The salient aspects of confidential information in Malaysia are as in Appendix 6.

PREPARING THE HARMONISATION WITH TRIPS BY YEAR 2000

To ensure TRIPS is fully enforced in Malaysia by year 2000, a Sub-Committee on TRIPS was established under the IPD, DOMTRADE to study and oversee Malaysia's obligation as well as implementation of the agreement. The members of the Sub-Committee are drawn from the public sector and related agencies, the private sector, academicians, trade associations, Non-Government Organisations (NGOs) and IP Associations. Subsequently 5 Working Groups were established to assist this Sub-Committee.

The 5 Working Groups are:

- Working Group on Trade Marks and Geographical Indications
- Working Group on Patents, Layout Designs, Industrial Designs, Undisclosed Information and Control of Anti-Competitive Practices
- Working Group on Copyright and Related Rights
- Working Group on Enforcement
- Working Group on General Provisions, Acquisition and Maintenance, Dispute Prevention and Settlement, Transitional Arrangement and Institutional Arrangement

All the Working Groups have completed their study and have submitted their findings and recommendations to DOMTRADE. The recommendations of the Sub-Committees, including promulgation of new laws and amendments of existing ones, are currently being acted upon by the IPD for implementation. Full compliance with TRIPS is expected by year 2000.

On the legislative front, new laws will have to be enacted on Neighbouring Rights, Layout Designs of Integrated Circuits and Plant Varieties. Amendments will also have to be made to the existing patent, trade mark, customs and trade description legislations.

Similarly, on the administrative and regulatory front, in order to be reliable and effective, DOMTRADE has automated its trademark office to ensure that search and opposition can be swiftly done. The Government will also allocate more manpower and financial allocation to streamline procedures for the implementation on existing and new IP laws. Currently, the Trademark Office is served by an HP 9000 computer system via 19 terminals for trademark administration. On manpower training, under the ASEAN EC Programme, IP examiners will continue to obtain world class training in accelerated examination so as to improve productivity and speed.

To ensure that IPR regime is well administered in Malaysia, and in consonance with international practices, DOMTRADE has set up the Institute of Intellectual Property (IIP) that will provide training to potential patent agents and officials from the government sector. The IIP, currently resident on the main campus of the National Institute of Public Administration at Bukit Kiara, conducts qualifying examinations for patent agents in Malaysia. This will augment training in IP that is currently conducted at the Masters level by 4 local universities.

DOMTRADE has also beefed up the Enforcement Unit to ensure full conformance of IPR laws and the Trade Description Act, 1972. Punitive action will be taken against all merchants and purveyors of counterfeits and pirated works. Currently, raids have been conducted on all commercial premises to ensure offenders are brought to book. These enforcement actions will be a permanent feature to further outlaw the illegal trade in IP before the current year closes and thereafter.

DOMTRADE also intends to provide sufficient training and exposure to all legal personnel, be those on the bench or the bar, so that they understand IP laws better and the need for protection so as to better administer "technology related" cases brought before the courts.

In order to ensure, Malaysia is at the fore-front in IP and technology development, DOMTRADE will continue to monitor IP development at national and international levels and in the formulation of policies, strategies and legislations with related regulatory agencies that will further improve IP management in Malaysia as well as in the promotion of inventiveness, innovation, creativity, R&D and international trade.

IMPLEMENTATION ISSUES

Even though Malaysia has taken all the necessary steps (particularly in form) towards full conformance with TRIPS, there is a visible need to improve IPR management and performance on all fronts. Malaysian authorities are thus monitoring all procedures and time-lines so as to better serve industry and inventors. In this, DOMTRADE will cut out all its non-productive activities and focus on the critical activities that will speed up its processes in IPR administration.

The issue of productivity and speed is a consuming concern at DOMTRADE. There is a definite need to ensure competent examiners with skill sets in adequate numbers to serve in the various branches of the IP office. Continuous training programmes and long term, human resources planning must be put in place so that IP management in Malaysia can attain world class. The performance of the IPD, as such, will be benchmarked regularly against best models of the world so that it will continue to excel in the field of IPR management.

Similarly, the enforcement and legal redress mechanisms must be given due attention so that infringers can be quickly apprehended and remedies appropriately and speedily dispensed with. The Malaysian authorities are thus currently studying these two aspects and the fine tuning of such mechanisms will be an on-going activity.

In order the break the habit of consuming pirated goods and cheap counterfeits amongst the consumer population, DOMTRADE will certainly be saddled with the arduous task of re-educating consumers so that they will no longer indulge in the purchase of such infringing items. Public promotion campaigns as such will have to be conducted periodically and definitely on a sustained basis so that piracy and counterfeiting will be kept at bay.

CONCLUSION

No amount of motherhood statements can help stamped out the piracy trade and counterfeit business if governments of the day in developing countries continue to be lackadaisical in their approach to IPR protection. In fact, the downside of such an approach will be the negative impact on research and development, indigenous technology development and trade. Apart from earning a notorious position on the WTO 'black list'; on the long run, it will stunt the economic and cultural development of these economies and affects the general well being of its citizens. The choice of a better tomorrow lies in their hands.

Looking ever forward, developing countries must continue to improve its lot particularly in an era where competitiveness and productivity rules the markets. As the approaching millennium beckons, all developing economies must put their house in order particularly so in IPR management so that their country will progress along with global prosperity as envisioned by the founding fathers of the WTO.

Appendix 1
INTELLECTUAL PROPERTY RIGHTS

Legislation/Applicable Legislations in Malaysia

Year	*Related Legislation/Development*
In Force	United Kingdom Design (Protection) Act, 1949 (Malaya) United Kingdom Design (Protection) Ordinance, Sabah) United Kingdom Design (Protection) Ordinance, Sarawak
1972	Trade Description Act, 1972 in force.
1976	Trademark Act, 1976 passed.
1983	Patents Act, 1983 was passed by Parliament Trademark Regulations, 1983 came into force.
1986	Patents (Amendment) Act, 1986 (amending the 1983 Act)
1987	New Copyright Act, 1987 (repealing Copyright Act,1969)
1988	Malaysia becomes a member of the Paris Convention
1989	Malaysia acceded to the Berne Convention
1990	Copyright (Amendment) Act, 1990 passed to be compatible with the Berne Convention for the Protection of Literary and Artistic Works
1995	Patents (Amendment) Act, 1995 and regulations thereunder in force.

Appendix 2
PATENTS

GOVERNING LEGISLATION

- Before 1 October 1986, patents were registered in the UK and were re-registered in Sabah and Sarawak.
- The Patents Act, 1983 as amended by the Patents (Amendment) Act 1986 came into force on 1 October 1986.
- Re-registered patents are deemed certificates of patents under the 1983 Act
- Patents (Amendment) Act, 1995 and the regulations thereunder is the current legislation in force.

WHAT IS PATENTABLE

- Patent law is a law designed to confer a monopoly on the creator of a novel invention. An invention is basically an idea which gives a practical solution to a specific problem in the field of technology and may either relate to a product or process.
- An invention is patentable if it is new, has an inventive step and has industrial application [Section 11 of the 1983 Act]

A certificate of utility will be provided for petty patents. It need not have to conform to the strict criteria qualification for patents.

WHAT IS NOT PATENTABLE

- Discovery, scientific theory and mathematical method.
- Plant or animal variety of essential biological process for the production of man-made living organisms, micro biological processes and the product of such micro organisms.

- Rule or method for doing business as in performing purely mental acts or playing games
- Method for the treatment of human or animal body.

DURATION OF PROTECTION

- Section 35 provides protection for 15 years from date of grant.
- A patent issued under earlier repealed Act, most specifically, the Registrar of UK Patents Act, 1951 will remain in force for as long as the original patent remains in force in the UK or until the expiration of 21 years from the date of application whichever, is earlier.

UTILITY INNOVATION (UI)

- Known also as petty patents or utility models, it includes any implement, product or process which is of practical utility by reason of its form, configuration, construction or composition.
- UI is deemed new if it has not been disclosed to the public in Malaysia, prior to filing date.

DURATION OF PROTECTION

5 years and renewable for two consecutive five year terms, if shown to be in commercial use in Malaysia.

RIGHTS OF THE OWNER OF PATENT

Exclusive right to:

- Exploit the invention
- Assign or transmit the patent
- Conclude license contracts

INFRINGMENT

An infringement is a violation of the monopoly rights conferred on a grant holder.

Commercial use of both product or process without permission of the grant holder is tantamount to infringement.

REMEDIES

Section 60 (1) of the Patents Act sets out the remedies available to a successful plaintiff. This include injunctions, damages and other legal remedy.

There is however, no criminal liability.

Appendix 3

TRADE MARKS

GOVERNING LEGISLATION

Trademark Act of 1976 and the Trademark Regulations, 1983 which came into force on 1 September 1983.

The Act is essentially formulated similar to the provisions of the UK Trade Marks Act, 1938

It unified trademark laws in Malaysia by centralising administrative and legal procedures.

Beginning 1 September 1983, a single trademark application to cover the whole of Malaysia can be filed at the Central Registry in Kuala Lumpur.

"MARKS" AND "TRADE MARKS"

Marks defined as:

- Including a device, brand, heading, label, ticket, name, signature, word, letter, numeral or any combination thereof.

  (The statutory definition of a *mark is wide enough* to *encompass almost* any *visual feature applied to goods.)*

A trade mark means:

- A mark used or proposed to be used,
- In relations to goods,
- For the purposes of indicating or (distinctiveness) so as to indicate a connection,
- In the course of trade between the goods and a person having the right as the proprietor or as registered user to use the mark [Section 3, 1976 Act].

WHAT MARKS ARE REGISTRABLE

- To qualify as a registrable mark, it should contain at least one of the following particulars

- The name of an individual, company or firm represented in a special or particular manner
- The signature of the applicant for registration or of some predecessor in his business
- An invented word or words
- A word having no direct reference to the character or quality of the goods not being, according to its ordinary meaning, a geographical name or surname

Any distinctive mark - the trademark is inherently adapted to distinguish. And by the reason of the use of the trademark in any other circumstances, the trademark is in fact adopted to distinguish.

A name, signature or word which is not described in the above paragraphs of sub-section 1 of Section 10 is not registrable in Part A of the Register unless it is by evidence shown to be distinctive.

WHAT MARKS ARE NOT REGISTRABLE

The 1976 Act contains specific prohibitions against registration. A mark is not registrable if it is a mark

- Which is likely to deceive or cause confusion to the public
- Which is contrary to law
- Which contains or comprises any scandalous or offensive matter [Section 14(a) and Section 14(b)]

Section 19 of the Act prohibits registration of a trademark in respect of any goods that is Identical with a trade mark belonging to a different proprietor and already registered in respect of the same goods or description of goods or so nearly resembling such a trade mark as is likely to deceive or cause confusion.

EXAMINATION PROCEDURE

- Two fold procedure.
- The mark is examined to determine if it is inherently registrable or non-registrable (Section 10).
- A search is conducted to ascertain any similar marks are registered or pending registration. If there are, objection will be raised under Section 19(1) and or Section 19(2).
- If not, the mark is advertised in the government gazette. If there is no opposition within two months, Registrar will request applicant will pay required fees and the registration certificate will be issued.
- Decision of the Registrar is subject to appeal in the High Court.

DURATION AND RENEWAL

Registration is valid for an initial period of 7 years [Section 32(1)] commencing from the date of application which when registered will be deemed to be the registration date and thereafter renewable for terms of 14 years.

PROTECTION OF RIGHTS OF TRADEMARK OWNERS

Relief prayed for includes restraining injunctions, delivery up for destruction or erasure of offending marks, damages and cost of proceedings.

- Criminal remedies: Fines not exceeding RM 100,000 or imprisonment not exceeding 3 years or both. For corporations, the fine is RM 250,000.

Appendix 4

INDUSTRIAL DESIGNS

GOVERNING LEGISLATION

Three Acts govern industrial design in Malaysia. These are:

1. The United Kingdom Designs (Protection) Act,1949 (Malaya)
2. The United Kingdom Designs (Protection) Ordinance (Sabah)
3. The United Kingdom Designs (Protection) Ordinance (Sarawak)

- The above 3 Acts provide for the registered proprietor of a design registered under the United Kingdom Registered Design Act, 1949 or any Act amending and substituting for it, to enjoy in the respective parts of Malaysia, "the like privileges and rights as though the Certificate of Registration had been issued with an extension" to these territories. As such, in substance, the law applicable in Malaysia in respect of Registered Designs is the law as applicable in the UK.
- Designs registered in the UK under the Registered Designs Acts 1949 of UK as amended by the UK Copyright, Designs and Patents Act, 1988 are automatically protected in Malaysia.

RIGHTS THAT ARE PROTECTED

- Industrial Design law is aimed to protect industrially exploited designs as opposed to inventions. Examples are:- ornamental and artistic features and designs of the article; both in two-dimensional drawing form and in the three dimensional object form.

WHAT DESIGNS ARE REGISTRABLE

Section 1 of the 1949 UK Act define

- A "design" as features of shape, configuration, pattern or ornament.
- The "design" is applied to an article by any industrial process or means.

- The "design" being features which in the finished article appeal to and judged solely by the eye.

The design must be new in Malaysia in that it must be original or novel.

WHAT DESIGNS ARE NOT REGISTRABLE

A "design" which includes a method or principle of construction or features of shape or configuration of an article which;

- Are dictated solely by the function which the article has to perform
- Are dependent upon the appearance of another article of which the article is intended by the author of the design to form an integral part is not registrable.

Also, a design which is the same as any design which before the date of application for registration been registered or published in respect of any article or differs only in such design in immaterial details or in features which are variants commonly used in the trade shall not be registrable.

DURATION OF PROTECTION

- Registration of a design takes effect on the date of registration as indicated on the certificate of registration.
- Protection is for a period of 5 years, subject to a renewal of two further 5-year periods.

  (15 years under the 1949 UK Act and 25 years under the 1988 UK Act.)

EFFECT OF REGISTRATION

The registration of a design gives to the registered proprietor the exclusive right in Malaysia to:

- Make or import for sale or for use for the purpose of any trade or business
- To sell, hire or offer for sale or hire any article in respect of which the design is registered.

The right extends to articles to which a design not substantially different from the registered design has been applied.

INFRINGEMENT

- Action can be brought only be a registered proprietor [Section 7(1) of the UK Act].
- Relief is in the form of Interim injunctions, damages and order for delivery and costs.
- Action under the Copyrights Act, in certain circumstances, is also possible.

COPYRIGHT PROTECTION IN RESPECT FOR INDUSTRIAL DESIGNS

- Copyrights Act, 1987 defines artistic works to include paintings, drawings, etchings and any three-dimensional works thereof and works of artistic craftsmanship including articles of applied handicraft and industrial art.
- In order to acquire copyright, an industrial design does not necessarily have to have any artistic quality. However, it must be original in character.
- To qualify for such protection, the author of such design should be at the time the work is being made, be a Malaysian citizen or a permanent resident in Malaysia.

Appendix 5
COPYRIGHTS

GOVERNING LEGISLATION

- The Copyright Act, 1987
- The Copyright (Amendment) Act, 1990

NATURE OF RIGHT

Copyright is the exclusive right to control in whole or for a substantive part of a work either in its original or derivative form.

In Malaysia, copyright confers exclusive right over

- The reproduction in any material form
- The performance, showing or playing to the public
- Broadcasting
- Communication by cable,
- Distribution of copies to the public.

OWNERSHIP OF COPYRIGHT

- Copyright is vested initially in the author.
- Exceptions in cases where it is conferred by agreement or if first owner is the Government or an international body.

DURATION OF COPYRIGHT

- The life of the author plus 50 years in the case of literary, musical or artistic works
- Copyright in sound recording, photograph, film and works of government will expire 50 years from the end of the calendar year in which the works was first published.

WORKS ELIGIBLE FOR COPYRIGHT

- Literary works (including computer programmes & published editions of literary works)
- Musical works
- Artistic works
- Films
- Sound recordings
- Broadcasts

CRITERION FOR PROTECTION

Must satisfy the three criteria of form, content and status.

Form

To be eligible for copyright, it must be written down, recorded or otherwise reduced to material form [Section 7(3)(b)].

Material form includes any form (visible or otherwise) of storage from which the work can be reproduced [Section 3].

Note: Copyright protection goes only to the particular expression of ideas and not to ideas themselves.

Content

Refers to the minimum content requirement to be satisfied for copyright protection eligibility.

- Literary, musical or artistic works: Sufficient effort must be expended to make the work original in character [Section 3(a) of 1987 Act] *(Original skill or labour in execution and not originality of thought)*

Status

Connection of work to a jurisdiction by a recognised connecting factor.

Pre-Berne Convention: (Before 1 October 1990)

Authors who were non-qualified persons [Section 3] were protected by the 1987 Act only if their works has been first published in Malaysia, either simultaneously or within 30 days of their first publication in a foreign country.

Post-Berne convention (From 1 October 1990)

Pursuant to regulations under Section 59A, Copyright (Amendment) Act, 1990,thc following categories of work originating from member countries of the Berne Convention is automatically protected in Malaysia.

- Literary works
- Musical works
- Artistic works

- Films & cinematography works
- Dramatic works

Further Protection via the Berne Convention

- Derivative works of musical, literary or artistic works shall be protected as original works without prejudicing original works.
- Definition of the word "author" need no longer mean a local author, an author who is a citizen, a resident author or a foreign author.
- The author or maker of a work must be a qualified person at the time when the work is made.

Definition of a Qualified Person (1987 Act)

(ll) Malaysian Citizen

(mm) Permanent citizen of Malaysia

(nn) Body corporate under Malaysian law

(oo) National or person of permanent residence in member countries of the Berne Convention

(pp) Body corporate under the laws of any member countries of Berne Convention

INFRINGEMENT

Infringement is deemed to have occurred when a person without license from a copyright owner does acts (or causing another to act) restricted by copyright under Section 3(1) of the Act which includes the following:

- The reproduction in any material form
- The performance, showing or playing to the public
- Broadcasting
- Communication by cable,
- Distribution of copies to the public by sale, rental, lease or lending.

Secondary infringement is also provided for under the Act. Without the consent or license of the owner, an infringement is deemed to have occurred if the purpose is for trade or in a manner prejudicial to the owner of copyright.

REMEDIES

Civil Action

- Whereby relief is in the form of damages & injunctions. Anton Pillar Order is also available.

Criminal Offences

- Under the 1987 Act, an offence under Section 41 is deemed a criminal offence if his actions are for purposes of trade.

Appendix 6
CONFIDENTIAL INFORMATION

GOVERNING LAW

- Not codified but based largely on English Common Law.

DEFINITION

- The law of confidence enables one party who imparts information in confidence to another to obtain relief against the recipient if the latter, without permission, uses the information or discloses it to third parties.
- Major source of the doctrine of breach of confidence is from the law relating to confidential information whereby information is the object of an obligation.
- Confidential information covers government secrets, trade secrets and artistic secrets.

RELIEF

- Types of information that may be protected range from government and public secrets, commercial and technical secrets and personal confidence.
- Relief is granted based on contract and breach of trust.

BREACH OF CONFIDENCEITRUST

To make out a case in an action of breach of confidence, the plaintiff is required to prove three elements. The three elements are:

- The information must have the necessary Quality of confidence.

  (Subject matter is not common knowledge or public domain material. Subject matter must be original).
- The information must have been imparted in circumstances importing a relationship of confidence.

(When the subject matter is discussed, the recipient must realise that the information is being imparted in circumstances imparting an obligation of confidence. Recipient owes an equitable obligation of confidence. Acid test is on fact.)

- There must be an unauthorized use of the information to the detriment of the party communicating it.

  (Proof of unauthorized *use is required. The information must definitively come from the plaintiff and not from other independent source or through reverse* engineering).

BREACH OF CONTRACT

Expressed and implied terms.

Expressed terms are by virtue of a contract.

Implied terms are determined as follows:

- Nature of the employment
- Nature of the information itself
- Confidentiality of the information conveyed
- Confidential information be isolated from other information.

DEFENCES

Available as follows:

- If the information itself does not contain any confidential information.
- That there exists no duty not to disclose as the information becomes part of the recipient's skill.
- The confidential information is not severable from the information that is not confidential.
- Public interest.
- Acquiescene and delay.

REMEDIES

- The remedies available for IPR are applicable to breach of confidence.
- Plaintiff in an action may sue for an injunction and for damages.

Appendix 7

FUNCTIONS OF THE INTELLECTUAL PROPERTY DIVISION, THE MINISTRY OF DOMESTIC TRADE AND CONSUMER AFFAIRS, MALAYSIA

- Provides facilities for filing of trademark, patent and utility innovation applications.
- Handles all the administrative matters relating to the processing of new trade mark, patent, utility innovation applications and trade mark post registration applications.
- Conduct search and examination on trademark, patent and utility innovation applications.
- Provides facilities for public search on matters related to trademark & patents.
- Reviews and updates the existing Copyright Act and formulates new Acts in compliance with international norms and practices.
- Provides facilities for filing industrial designs applications.
- Will handle administrative details associated with the processing of industrial design applications in the near future.
- Handles queries on intellectual property.

11

INTELLECTUAL PROPERTY SYSTEM OF MONGOLIA

Embassy of Mongolia

(Embassy of Mongolia in New Delhi, India)

GENERAL REMARKS

Mongolia is a democratic country with a parliament governance and market economy. The Mongolian Constitution, adopted in 1992, established a uni-cameral legislature and a directly elected President with relatively limited powers. The Prime Minister is nominated by the President and approved by the Parliament. The present majority in the Parliament is held by the Mongolian People's Republic Party. There are numerous registered political parties in Mongolia, of which four currently hold seats in the present Parliament.

Today, Mongolia opened its doors to international investors and traders and is actively broadening its relations with its trading partners in the West and the East. Mongolia receives aid through a group of donor countries and multilateral organizations, as well as loans from international finance institutions such as World Bank and Asian Development Bank. In May 1997, Mongolia joined the World Trade Organization and liberalized tariffs on import customs duties.

Mongolia has undertaken a massive program of privatization. The first phase of the privatisation of state property, covering small and medium size enterprises and livestock, has been successfully completed. In May 1997, Mongolia began to privatize dwellings free of charge.

Native Industries

Production of cashmere, skins and leathers, furs and animal hair, mining (including copper, coal, molybdenum, iron, phosphates, tin, nickel, zinc, wolfram, fluorspar, gold and uranium) and construction.

Major Export Items

Copper, molybdenum, fluorspar concentrates, camel wool, cashmere and leather garments.

Major Import Items

Oil products, machinery, equipment, gasoline, construction materials.

BACKGROUND OF INTELLECTUAL PROPERTY SYSTEM

Foundation of intellectual property system in Mongolia is laid back in 40s step by step. The first legislative act relating to a protection of industrial property was enacted in 1944. This document applied mainly to encourage innovators and inventors.

Subsequent steps have been taken in the course of running the society to improve the foundation of the patent legislation. In 1960 the Statute on Inventions and Innovations was enacted, and in 1970 it was renewed as the Statute on Discoveries, Invention and Innovations. In 1967, the Statute on Trademarks and Appellation of Origin was adopted. This act was revised twice and in 1987 was renewed as the Statute on Trademarks. The Statute on Industrial Designs was enacted in 1976. All these Statutes had been enacted in compliance with the corresponding provisions of the Civil Code of Mongolia.

Prior to the establishment of the Mongolian Patent Office in October 1990, industrial property activities were under the responsibility of corresponding Departments of different government agencies such as the State Planning Commission since 1945, the State Board on Standardization since 1960, the State Committee for Science and Technology since 1971, the Ministry for National Development since 1990. The National Copyright Office was established in 1993 under the Ministry of Culture.

In September 1996, by the decision of the Government of Mongolia the Intellectual Property Office of Mongolia (IPOM) has been formed by combining the Patent and Trademark Office and National Copyright Office.

Since 1996 up to now, IPOM, the Government Implementing Agency under the Ministry of Justice and Home Affairs is the main body to implement government policies in the field of intellectual property and to represent the government in the international treaties to which the country part of.

PATENT

Legal Basis

"Patent Law of Mongolia" No.101 (601)/1993 (amended as of December 19, 1996 and May 21, 1999).

Definition of an "invention" given in the law is an absolutely new solution that relates to a product or process, that has been created for the first time, and essence of which is disclosed on the basis of a law of nature.

Patentability

A patent can be granted for a product or a process, which is absolutely new, involves an inventive step and is industrially applicable. An invention shall be considered as involving an inventive step, if it is not obvious to a person skilled in the art. An invention shall be considered industrially applicable, if it can be made or used in industry.

Not Patentable

(a) discoveries, scientific theories and mathematical methods; b) computer programs and algorithms; c) schemes, rules or methods for doing business, performing mental acts or playing games; d) solutions that are contrary to public health or environmental protection; e) methods of treatment and diagnosis, or prophylaxis of human and animal diseases; f) biological processes for the production of animals or plants other than microorganisms.

Protection

A patent is granted by the state authority which certifies the recognition of the given solution as an invention, the owner thereof having the exclusive right to exploit it for a fixed period of time.

Priorities

In accordance with the Paris Convention.

Validity

Twenty years, running from the patent granting date applicable to the PCT International applications.

Membership in International Conventions

- Paris Convention, Stockholm Act, since April 21, 1985.
- WIPO, since 1979.
- PCT, since May 27,1991.
- Strasbourg Agreement Concerning the International Patent Classification, since 2000.
- TRIPS Agreement, since June 1,1997.

TRADE AND SERVICE MARKS

Legal Basis

- Law on Trademarks and Geographical Indications, May 2, 2003.
- Trademark, collective mark, certification mark and geographical indication are protectable under the Law.
- Trademark is defined as a distinctive expression used by a natural or a legal person, engaged in the manufacturing of goods or the provision of services, in order to distinguish the goods or services from those of others.

- Collective mark defined means a trademark used by manufacturers and service providers under the associated control.
- Certification mark as a trademark authorized to be used by others, when its owner attests quality, method of production and other characteristics of certain goods or services.
- Geographical indication defined as the geographical name of a country, region or locality, which identifies a good as originating therein, where a given quality, reputation or other characteristic of the good is essentially attributable to its geographical origin.

Trademarks may be expressed in words, figures, letters, numerals, three-dimensional configurations, colors, sounds, scents or any combinations thereof.

The followings are not considered as a trademark: generally known terms, shapes or any signs, letters or numerals devoid of distinctive character; generic names of the goods or services; words or figures indicating the quantity, size, weight, quality, purpose, price, or place, time or method of manufacturing; and ordinary shapes of goods or their packaging.

The followings are not registered as a trademark: denominations that consist of, or identical with, or similar to, the national emblems, flags or other State symbols of Mongolia or foreign countries, or official emblems, the full or abbreviated names of international organizations, governmental or non-governmental organizations; reproductions of the full or abbreviated names, portraits, pictures or signatures of famous persons, if used without the consent of those persons or their heirs; reproductions of the names, pseudonyms, portraits or pictures of historical persons of Mongolia or suggested names directly related thereto, if used in a manner disparaging them; reproductions of names or representations of Mongolian historical or cultural monuments, if used in a manner disparaging them; signs identical with, or similar to the decorations, medals or other awards, or to official signs and ha lmarks indicating control and warranty; indications, the content of which is contr ry to public order or morality; indications liable to deceive or mislead consumers as to the nature, quality, geographical origin or other characteristics of the goods or serv ces; and geographical map or a location shown on the geographical map. • Term of the tra emark registration is 10 years and renewable at the expiration of the protection term. • **Membership in International Conventions** • □Paris Convention, Stockholm Act, since April 21, 1985. •□•□Madrid Agreement for the International Registration of Marks (1891), as revised in Stockholm (1967), as of April 21, 1985. •□•□Protocol Rela ing to the Madrid Agreement Concerning the International Registration of Marks, since 2000. ••••Nice Agreement Concerning the International Classification of Goo s and Services for the Purposes of the Registration of Marks since 2000 • **INDUSTRIAL D SIGNS** • **Legal Basis** • "Patent Law of Mongolia" No. 101 (601)/1993 (amended as of Dec mber 19, 1996 and May21, 1999). • Industrial design defined as a new outward app arance of the article consisting i

the secularity of forms, drawings and ornaments, composition of colors capable of being produced by industrial means. Industrial designs may be three-dimensional, plane or combined.

Variants

Several variants can be protected if they refer to the same class of international classification and do not essentially differ from each other.

Not Registrable

When conflicting with the requirements of public laws and-morality or consisting of state flags, armorial bearings and emblems of international organizations. Priority: priority of an application filed in a country, which is party to the Paris Convention may be claimed.

Conditions for Protection

The description of the design must state the following in comparison with already known designs: (a) novelty of the industrial design; (b) technical and aesthetical qualities of the design; (c) the suitability of its production by industrial means.

Validity

Ten years running from the granting date.

Membership in International Conventions

- Paris Convention, Stockholm Act, since April 21, 1985.
- Hague Agreement concerning the International Deposit of Industrial Designs, since 1997.
- Locarno Agreement Establishing an International Classification for Industrial Designs, since 2000.

COPYRIGHT

Legal Basis

Law of Mongolia on Copyright as of 22 June 1993.

Definition of protected works: the subject matter of copyright shall include the following works irrespective of their content, purpose, form, mode of creation or availability to the public:

- Literary works in the scientific or literary domain whether verbal or written;
- Musical works;
- Graphic works and works of applied art;
- Works of architecture and construction design;
- Choreographic works, works of contortionists and pantomime;
- Dramatic works;
- Cinematographic works and all works expressed by a process analogous to cinematography;

- Photographic works and all works expressed by a process analogous to photography;
- Plans, sketches, designs, and models relative to the scientific and technical domain;
- Computer programs;
- Encyclopedia, dictionary other database compilation that composes an intellectual creation by its content and purpose.
- Derived works such as adaptation, translation, arrangements of musical and other artistic works based on pre-existing works
- Any other works expressing the intellectual creative activity of the author

Membership in International Conventions

- Berne Convention for the Protection of Literary and Artistic, Works, since 1998.
- WIPO Copyright Treaty, since May 2002
- WIPO Performance and Phonograms Treaty, since May 2002

Contact Information

The related information and soft copies of the national laws and legislation in the sector and there translations can be found at the site www.ipom.mn or in the digital library of WIPO www.wipo.int.

The address of the Intellectual Property Office of Mongolia:

IPO Mongolia

Baga-toiruu 49

Ulaanbaatar 46

Mongolia

Tel.: +976 11 329671

Fax: +976 11 327638

12

INTELLECTUAL PROPERTY RIGHTS AND EXISTING LEGAL PROVISION IN NEPAL

R.M.S. Malla

(Under Secretary, Ministry of Law and Justice and Mr. K.N. Poudyal, Law Officer, Ministry of Science and Technology, Singdhadurbar, Kathmandu, Nepal)

INTRODUCTION

Nepal is one of the least developed country of 20 million people with per capita income of US $ 210 only. Its development plan heavily depends on foreign investment and in Nepal it is increasingly being recognized that national development goals can be achieved only through technological innovations. A strong and sound IPR system will be needed to encourage and promote inventive and innovative activities for the adequate protection against infringement. Thus a well structured, modern intellectual property right system which provides rights which can be properly enforced is a great stimulus to innovation and which also encourage foreign investor or enterprises to invest or to transfer the proper technology for the economic development.

The term intellectual property rights is used to protect the intangible asset for the promotion and development of inventive and innovative activities of the human mind, the human intellect. Intellectual Property comprises of two main components, namely (i) industrial property and (ii) copyright. Industrial property consists mainly of patents, industrial designs and trademarks and copyright relates to artistic creations, such as poems, novels, music, paintings, cinematographic works etc.

In Nepal, for the first time the intellectual property rights was legally established in 1937, when the Patent, Design and Trademarks Act was enacted. This Act was substituted by the Patent Design and Trademarks Act of 1965, which extended the provision of protection to foreign national as well. This Act has undergone an amendment in 1987 and this amended version is still regulating the existing industrial property protection system of Nepal. And for the protection of literary and artistic creation the Copy Right Act, 1965 was promulgated for the first time. Besides, these two laws on INTELLECTUAL PROPERTY RIGHTS system there are some other laws which are related with the INTELLECTUAL PROPERTY RIGHTS system and enforcing in Nepal are the Industrial Enterprises Act, 1992. Foreign Investment and Technology Transfer Act, 1992, Compnay Act, 1997 and Export Import (Control) Act, 1957.

The Department of industry is the responsible authority of His Majesty's Government of Nepal for the administration of industrial property in the country as per the Patent, Design and Trademark Act, 1965. And the Ministry of youth, Sports and Culture is the responsible for the administration of copyright. All kinds of operating tasks of industrial property and copyright are carried out by Department of Industry and Ministry of Youth, Sports and Culture respectively under the policy directions of HMG/N. A number of professional organizations are directly or indirectly involved in the IPR protection system in Nepal. These include the Royal Nepal Academy for science and Technology (RONAST), the National Agriculture Research centre (NARC), the Royal Nepal Academy, the Federation of Nepal Chamber of Commerce and Industry (FNCCI) and the Nepal Chamber of Commerce.

EXISTING LEGAL PROVISION

Industrial Property

Industrial property principally deals with the protection of patents, trademarks and industrial designs, and the repression of unfair competition. These areas have certain features in common in as such as protection granted for patents, trademarks and industrial designs in the form of exclusive rights of exploitation are concerned. The repression of unfair competition is not concerned with exclusive rights, but is directed against act of competition contrary to honest practices.

Industrial property administration system is not fully developed in Nepal likely to most of the developed countries of the world. The existing patent, Design and Trademarks Act is inadequate. It does not cover all aspects of industrial property protection system and the provision for enforcement measures is also inadequate and weak. Thus the Act promulgated in 1965 has never really been enforced in an effective manner. The basic reasons for these arte the very low level of country's economic development and the lack of systematic support and protection for inventive and innovative activities, including research and development.

The provisions made in the existing Act has specifically mentioned about the definition of patent, design and trademark, right on the property, application, examination and registration procedures, areas which cannot be protected, tenure of protection, and penalty and compensation against the violation of the rights and infringement. The provision of the Act also covers the protection of foreign industrial property in the territory of the Kingdom of Nepal.

Patent System in Nepal

As per the Nepalese law patents are legal rights granted for new inventions employing scientific and technical knowledge. The subject of patent, which involves scientific and legal issues, is relatively complicated as compared with other species of intellectual property like designs, trademarks and copyrights. A patent confers on its holders the exclusive right for a limited period, the right of use of invention or to authorize other. The period of protection is seven years and may be renewed for two subsequent periods of sever years each. The application for the grant of a patent should be submitted with full disclosure of invention and in addition it also requires to state the name, address and the profession of the inventor, the description of inventions evidence of right over patent if the applicant is not the inventor, method of operation or utilization of the patent and the principles or formula behind the invention if applicable. Upon receipt of the application for the registration of patent, Department of Industry may consult with the experts in the related field like RONAST, NARC, TU to ascertain novelty and desirability for registration. Patent registered in any other country may be registered without any examination upon submission of certified copy of the certificate of registration.

A patent shall not be registered on the following conditions:

- If it is already registered in the name of others
- If the patent is not invented by the applicant and he has not acquired the right from the inventor.

The Department of Industry has the right to cancel the registration of patents provided that reasonable opportunity has been given to patents for the explanation.

Trademarks

A trademark is a visual symbol in the form of a word, device, or a lable applied to an article of manufacture of commerce with a view to indicate the purchasing member of the public about the origin of the manufacture for the goods affixed with that mark. It distinguishes such goods from the goods manufactured by other in the trade.

In Nepal trademarks are protected by the Patent, Design and Trademarks Act, 1965. The right of ownership under trademarks is obtained only by registration and the registration is subject to examination. In accordance with the provision of Nepalese Law trademarks are registered for a period of seven years from the date of registration and may be renewed any number of times of subsequent periods of seven years at a time on the payment of prescribed fee. The application for the registration of a trademark must include:

- An application in a prescribed format witnessed by two persons.
- A copy of the registration certificate of the firm or company providing the goods or services.
- Four copies of the sample of the trademark, if the trademark is a sign, a symbol or a picture.
- A letter for the nomination of attorney, where applicable.

The registration of trademarks of foreign origin is based on the registration in the home country and a copy of the certificate of registration needs to be submitted. The Department of Industry examines the sample marks submitted to ascertain similarity and if the submitted mark is found to be distinctly different, a decision to grant registration is made. The Department has right to cancel the registration of any mark if it is not used within one year of its registration. An infringement of trademark or violation of any provision of the Act with regards to trademark may result in the payment of a fine upto Rs. 1000/- and confiscation of all the materials related with such offence.

Industrial Designs

A design is an idea or conception as to features of shape, configuration, pattern or ornament applied to an article. The industrial design must have sense of sight and depends upon shape, pattern or colour of the products. It must be new and industrially reproducible.

In Nepal industrial designs are protected by the Patent, Design and Trademarks Act, 1965. the application for the registration of industrial design is subject to examination by the Department of Industry. In accordance with the provision of Nepalese Law designs are registered for a period of five years from the date of registration and may be renewed for two more terms of five years. The registration of a design of foreign origin is also based on foreign or home registration. An infringement of design or violation of any provision of the Act with regards to industrial design may result in the payment of a fine upto Rs. 800/- and confiscation of all the materials related with such offence.

Any industrial property that causes adverse effect to the health, conduct or morale of the people or to the national interest is not registered in Nepal After registration, the patent needs to be published in the national gazette. The design and trademark may also published after registration any person can make a complaint against the registration with 35 days of the publication. The Department of Industry will take necessary action through examination of such complaint. Industrial property registered in other country are not protected in Nepal unless it is registered in Nepal.

The existing Patent, Design and Trademark Law has not dealt with the protection relating to Geographical indication and protection against unfair competition. The Patent Design and Trademark Act, 1965 does not contain any provision on plant variety protection and layout design of interested circuits.

COPYRIGHT SYSTEM IN NEPAL

Copyright is basically the right to copy and make use of literary, dramatic, musical, artistic works, cinematographic films, records and broadcast. Copyright is a proprietary right and comes into existence as soon as the work is created. Copyright system in Nepal exist since the enactment of the Copyright Act 1965. The main provision mentioned in the Copyright Act are acquisition of copyrights, transfer, registration and licensing. In Nepal copyright protection is available only through the registration of the work with the registrar of the copyright. The registered work is regarded valid throughout the life of the author and continues for 50 years after his death. Transfer of copyright is permitted wholly or partially. Legal provision is inadequate and enforcement is even poor. The registration is compulsory but the number of registered copyright is very few.

Constraining Factors

The existing Patent, Design and Trademark Act, 1965 has never really been enforce in an effective manner. Much of the failure of the existing Act has to do with the fact that it failed to fuel inventions and innovations. Number of applications for the grant of patents and industrial designs in Nepal is very low. Only two or three applications, on an average are received annually. Only 43 patents and 27 designs have been registered in the last 62 years after the establishment of industrial property protection system in Nepal and 14231 Trademarks have been registered till March 1999.

In Nepal, the factors which could have helped, to a certain extent, to alleviate the intellectual property rights and economic development situation were rarely given an opportunity to come into play. The country has hardly ever had a clear strategy for the encouragement of inventive and innovative activity. For the development of inventive and innovative activity, characteristics and interrelationship of both these factors are to be understood not only by the producer and users of such inventions but also by the policy planners and decision makers.

Nepal needs a firm infrastructure in the communication sector to make the information public so as to ultimately motivate the people for wider application of new innovations. A good communication system is prerequisite for wider adoption of inventive and innovative activities.

The country also lacks in self-motivated and sustainable research institutions for inventive and innovative activity.

The existing Act lacks in the following provisions for the smooth and effective implementation of the IPR System:

- It has not covered all aspects of industrial property such as utility model, geographical indications, different kinds of marks, repression of unfair competition.
- Terminologies of various industrial property are not adequately defined.
- Lack of opportunity for the opposition and hearing before the registration or grant of particular industrial property.
- Penalties to repress infringement and unfair practices are not sufficient
- Examination and search criteria for the grant of a particular industrial property are not well stated.
- Hnauthorized exploitation of work specially in the field of arts, handicrafts and folk lore is taking place.
- Weak co-ordination within the concerned agencies has hindered the effective implementation. The organizational structure and enforcement system needs to be strengthened.
- Nepal is yet to enter international agreement relating to intellectual property.

ACTIONS TO BE TAKEN

For the improvement of the administration of the IPR System in Nepal, the following line of actions will prove to be helpful:-

- Strengthen the legal framework.
- Review and strengthen the organization
- Create public awareness.
- Develop manpower.
- Support inventive and innovative activities.
- Streamline the process and procedures.

CONCLUSION

Country's economic development is being increasingly associated with the ability to develop relevant technology and adapt such technology for economic production. Thus it is increasingly being recognized that national development goals can be achieved through technological innovation and which cannot be realized without appropriate support programmes which provide incentives for making investments. Therefore, a strong and sound IPR System is needed to encourage foreign investor or enterprises to invest or to transfer the proper technology for the economic development. And, for this the legislation relating to IPR System needs a major amendment to address the shortcoming and also meet the international standard including the requirement of TRIPS.

13

Intellectual Property Rights and Trade Related Intellectual Property Systems in Nepal

Fanindra Prasad Neupan

(Professor of Entomology and Dr. Keshar Man Bajracharya, Academician, Royal Nepal Academy of Science and Technology, New Baheshwor, Kathmandu, Nepal)

INTRODUCTION

This paper is concerned with the problems and prospects of developing as well as managing a suitable Intellectual Property Right (IPR) System in Nepal. IPR has become an important issue for all the countries including Nepal mainly due to economic liberalization and trade globalization to which our country has subscribed fully. Moreover. IPR if property capitalized through research and development in all aspects of economy and environment, will enable Nepal to shed her shackles of ignorance and poverty. However, due to the lack of advanced knowledge and understanding in scientific inventions, commercialization and international trading. Nepal is unable yet to develop an appropriate system of IPR in the country. To that extent we would like to include a brief country background and the IPR status in the context to which IPR problems and prospects are seen or experienced in Nepal.

COUNTRY BACKGROUND

Nepal is a small landlocked (China in the north and India on the other three sides) country in the Central Himalayas. Although small, Nepal has almost all the types of climates and continental natural and agro-ecological zones. This panorama of natural and cultural differences is brought about due to the altitudinal variations from the tropical plains, called the Terai with less than 100 meters msl through the subtropical Siwaliks hills and valleys (700 meters msl average), the Mid-land regions (1500 meters msl average) and the High Mountain Region (2000-4000 meters) to the High Himalayas with dozens of peaks above 7000 meters including the world's highest mountain, the Mount Everest at 8848 meters (CBS, 1995). Nepal had a monarchical system of government until 1990. Since then the country has a constitutional monarchy with multiparty system. The government has been somewhat ustable probably due to the teething problem of the new system.

Majority of the people (above 800/f) in Nepal are dependent on subsistence agriculture which provides about 43% of the national GDP (CBS, 1995). About 85% people live in the rural areas.

The major industries in Nepal include small and medium factories of sugar, jute, cement, cotton and synthetic cloth, tobacco, matches, carpet, garment, medicine and factories related to agriculture and forestry. The total number of establishments up to 1991/92 was 4271 with an employment of 223463 people (CBS, 1995). Tourism is another prosperous area. Handicrafts including gold and silver ornaments, wood and stone carving, metal sculpture, etc. are important products of Nepal.

The per capital income is about US$ 220 which is low. However, there is no dire poverty of landlessness and homeless as in some other South Asian Countries.

There are 20217 Primazy, 4376 Lower Secondary and 2242 Secondary Schools and five Universities in Nepal. There ate five technical institutes in the following areas: Agriculture and animal sciences, Engineering, Medicine, forestry and Science and Technology. The literacy rate is about 32%.

Nepal with its unique physical and climatic variations, is very rich in biodiversity. So far 9955 species of plants have been identified. Of the total flowering flora, 5% are endemic to Nepal and about 30% are endemic to the Himalayas (Shakya, 1999).

Research is in infancy in Nepal. Research activities are being carried out mainly by government departments and government supported semi-autonomous bodies such as Nepal Agricultural Research Council (NARC) and Royal Nepal Academy of Science and Technology (RONAST). Very little research is being carried out by the universities. However, there are altogether 80-90 agencies and institutions involved in the areas of research and development (R&D). Around 2000 scientists and technologists are involved in R&D. The low output realized in R&D is mainly due to the following reasons:

- The investment in the area of research is very low (only about 0.1% of the total GDP)
- There is no incentive to people involved in this area.
- Many foreign qualified people are not returning home and some experienced senior S&T persons have left or are leaving the country.

Nepal has foreign trade mainly with India and other countries. The imports far exceed the exports. In 1993/94 the export (f.o.b.) was equivalent to NRs 19417.9 million against an import of NRs 52433.6 million (CBS, 1995).

STATUS OF INTELLECTUAL PROPERTY RIGHTS IN NEPAL

Nepal's Membership with International Organizations Related to IPR

Nepal has become a member of WIPO. But it has not yet obtained the membership of the World Trade Organization (WTO) for which it has been trying.

Legislations Related to IPR

Intellectual Property Right (IPR) is a new concept for Nepal and many people are ignorant about it. The following acts are available in Nepal which are related to IPR:

Patents, Design and Trademark Act

This act was promulgated in 1937 which provided IPR protection to only Nepalese nationals. It was revised in 1965 and provided protection to both Nepalese and foreign nationals. It is again amended in 1987. Since this act does not cover all the aspects of industrial property protection system and the provision for enforcement measures are also inadequate and weak, a comprehensive Industrial Property Act is in the process of enactment (Acharya, 1998).

Copyright Act

This act was enacted in 1965 with the following provisions: acquisition of copyrights, transfer of registration and licensing. Copyright protection is available through the registration of the work which is valid throughout the life of the author and also continues for 50 years after his/her death. Transfer of copyright is permitted wholly or partially.

On the whole the legal provision to IPR is inadequate. In Nepal, the current statistics on the total number of patents (44) designs (26) and trademarks (9387) are unmistakable proof of that inadequacy. The details are presented in Table 13.1.

Table 13.1: Number of Registered Patents, Designs and Trademarks in Nepal

Time	*Type of IPR*								
	Patent			*Design*			*Trademark*		
	National	*Foreign*	*Total*	*National*	*Foreign*	*Total*	*National*	*Foreign*	*Total*
Up to Mid–April, 1993	15	21	36	3	15	18	3283	1998	5284
1993–94	–	–	–	–	1	1	445	189	634
1994–95	–	1	1	–	1	1	441	332	743
1995–96	1	–	1	–	1	1	404	617	1024
1996–91	1	2	3	–	3	3	512	418	928
1991–98	–	3	3	–	2	2	391	389	780
Total	**17**	**27**	**44**	**3**	**23**	**26**	**5446**	**3441**	**9387**

Source: Personal communications from Narendra K. Shrestha, Deputy Attorney General.

Awareness and Information Related to IPR

In this area some initiatives have been taken which are described below:

- A few workshops, seminars and meetings were organized on IPR in the past.
- Dr. G. Tyasarajan., representative of COSTED, delivered a lecture on IPR at RONAST in January 1997.
- A one-day seminar on IPR issues was organized during the Third Science and Technology Conference of RONAST in March 1999.
- UNIDO and WIPO have assisted in conducting workshops and seminars on patent and copyrights.
- Many persons from the ministries of Commerce Industries and other Government agencies/departments have participated on the subjects,

In spite of the above efforts, the country is unable to obtain benefits mainly due to lack of firm commitment on the part of the government as well as follow-up in assigning responsibility and authority to an interdisciplinary task force body for formulating an appropriate IPR system in the country.

In the past Nepal had felt the need of only a few agencies to manage the subjects of patent trademarks and copyrights. Accordingly, patent trademark administration was assigned to the MOI and that of the copyright to the National Library. In those days occasions to manage patent and copyright issues were few and far. Now that many other subjects including electronics and electric circuits, computer prognmming, arts and handicraft designs, audio and visual cassettes, etc. are involved in patent and copyrights, we need more complex and pervading IPR institutions. A few cases of infringement in copying of audio tapes have perplexed the law endorcement agencies like courts the police authority and other with respect to proper development and management of a suitable IPR system in the country. These issues when such "Intellectual" goods are also exported as in the case of the traditional designs in carpets and other handicrafts, could become more difficult to handle. Moreover, when we also include export and import of living organizations including plants animals and micro-organisms under IPR in general and trade related intellectual property rights (TRIPS) in particu1ar, it will indeed become an overwhelming task for Nepal.

When viewed in these perspectives it seems necessary to include under IPR almost all the government agencies and other non-government organizations as well as private firms that are involved in agriculture, industry, arts and crafts, biodiversity resources, R&D agencies, trading firms as well as law makers and law enforcing agencies in order to develop and manage a new system of IPR in Nepal.

PROBLEMS AND PROSPECTS OF IPR SYSTEM

Problems in Development/Management of an IPR Aystem

As stated earlier, IPR system is new to Nepal and there are only few people who know about it. Also there is inadequate legislation and that too without proper authority to inforce it. The general problems are further outlined below:

Political Immaturity and Uncertainty

Nepal is experiencing with a constitutional monarchy with multiparty democratic system very recently (less than a decade). The major political parties have yet to learn to run a government by a party with full majority in the parliament or by a coalition government in case of a hung parliament. Matters like IPR remained unattended by the government authorities under uncertainty of the government.

Bureaucratic Apathy

Several bureaucrats occupying key positions in the government have attended international meetings, seminars and workshops on IPR. But when they returned they did not show any interest or enthusiasm on IPR.

Lack of Vision and Mission Among the Decision Makers

Similarly, the decision makers did not have vision and mission on the area like IPR.

Lack of Proper Implementation of Adopted Policies and Plans

Whatever policies, plans and legislations have been made, they are not being implemented properly.

Lack of Monitoring and Evaluation

Monitoring and evaluation are indispensable tools for assessing the effectiveness of any action that the government starts. The nation should learn lessons and improve the future steps through these tools. In Nepal there is a conspicuous lack of monitoring and evaluation system.

IPR Potentiality for Sustainable Socio-economic and Environmental Development

IPR if properly implemented in Nepal, has a tremendous potentiality for sustainable socio-economic and environmental development. Some of the prospects in this area are mentioned below:

Varied Natural Ecosystems and their Rich Biodiversity

Due to varied ecosystems, different kinds of crops and other vegetations as well as animals can be raised in Nepal and exported to needy countries. The rich biodiversity could be exploited for various. uses.

Hard Working People

The people of Nepal are generally sincere and hard working. Our farmers, people involved in arts and handicraft, natural resource users and managers, scientists, students and others. If TRIPS are properly formulated and executed, the people mentioned above would contribute a lot for the socioeconomic development of the country.

Low Wage Rate

The wage rate in Nepal is low as compared to other SAARC countries. Hence, materials produced in Nepal would be cheaper for sale in the competitive world market under the rational IPR system.

Rich Indigenous Knowledge

Nepal is rich in indigenous knowledge and traditions. This knowledge could be used for the management and use of our rich biodiversity for export as well.

Favorable International and Bilateral Donors

The international and bilateral donors including WIPO, WTO etc. are sympathetic to help Nepal in formulating and promoting a suitable IPR regime.

SUGGESTIONS

Since IPR and TRIPS have become very complex issues in this age of trade globalization we have to compete with the global market for our survival. Hence IPR and TRIPS systems should be developed and utilized properly. For doing so a multidisciplinary task force on these areas should be formed with appropriate supports from the government organization private firms and donor agencies.

CONCLUSION

IPR is a new concept for Nepal where IP professionals, national laws, policies and instruments as well as proper institutions are lacking. There is a great threat of piracy of valuable biological materials as well as traditional knowledge. Hence. Nepal needs to develop its infrastructure, rules and laws to protect IPR in related areas. For resolving these problems, a multidisciplinary task force on these areas should be formed as soon as possible with appropriate supports from the government, industries and donor agencies.

REFERENCES

1. Acharya. B. B. 1999. *Intellectual Property Rights in the Kingdom of Nepal.* Paper Presented at the Third National Conference on Science and Technology, March 8-1, 1999, organized by Royal Nepal Academy of Science and Technology (RONAST), Kathmandu, Nepal.
2. CBS, 1995. *Statistical Yearbook of Nepal,* HMG, National Planning Commission Secretariat, Control Bureau of Statistics (CBS), Kathmandu, Nepal.
3. Shakya. P. R. 1999, *Handling Floral Diversity of Nepal.* Paper presented at the Third National Conference on Science and Technology. March 8-11, 1999. Organized by Royal Nepal Academy of Science and Technology (RONAST). Kathmandu, Nepal.

14

Development and Present Status of Copyright and Related Rights in Pakistan

Syed Ali Tallae

(Deputy Electronics Advisor (DAE), Saheed-I-Millat Secretariat, Ministry of Science and Technology, Islamabad, Pakistan)

The Pakistan Copyright Ordinance, 1962, which is in force at present has so far been amended twice by Copyright (Amendment) Acts of 1973 and 1992. The law contained therein provides adequate provisions for the protection and enforcement of copyrights and covers various fields of copyrights such as original literary works (including compilations and computer programmes), artistic works, audio-visual works, sound recordings, cinematographic works (including video films of every kind), broadcasts, translations and publisher's rights in typographical arrangement of published work, performers rights are not protected under Copyright Law, however, they can enforce their rights under the law of contract in pursuance of the terms and conditions of the agreements entered into by them with any concerned party or broadcasting organizations. In the area of collective administration, performing rights societies and author's organizations can be formed in the private sector, but those are either non-existent or non-functional at present. The law, however, provides for overseeing their functioning and determining the objections and disputes with regard to payment of royalties, fees and charges between the contracting parties.

Copyright protection has also been extended to the works originating in foreign countries which are members of the International Copyright Conventions *i.e.* Berne Convention, 1886, and Universal Copyright Convention, 1952 of which Pakistan is also a member/signatory since 1948, and 1955 respectively. Thus the protection is available to the foreign nationals (authors, artists and musicians ete.) under the above Conventions in like manner as the works originating in Pakistan. Accordingly, in pursuance of the powers conferred by Section 54 of the Ordinance, the Government of Pakistan has issued the International Copyright Order, 1968, the schedule whereof giving list of Member countries of Berne Union, Universal Copyright Convention and now of WTO has recently been updated. Pakistan has also entered into TRIPS agreement in compliance of which the legislative amendment exercise is being undertaken now-a-days. The implications and complications of two new international treaties on copyright and neighbouring rights, viz; WIPO Copyright Treaty 1996 and WIPO Performers and Phonograms Treaty, 1996 which have been concluded in consequence of diplomatic conference held in December 1996 are still to be comprehended fully. Pakistan, still in the infancy of her scientific and technological development in the new areas of copyright and neighbouring rights, such as digital and internet technology, multimedia and cyberspace etc. is to wait and see the outcome and experience of other developing and developed countries in coming decades before acceding to these treaties. The dissemination about new information technologies needs to be made available locally possibly with the assistance of international agencies like WIPO or other non-govermental agencies. At present internet is being used on a very limited scale in Pakistan. The Government has, however, constituted a task force and established some institutions on information technology. This context experience is also to be gathered out of the application of the provisions of TRIPS Agreement especially relating to database in coming decades.

The copyright is a vested right and provisions of registration under the copyright law have been made so as to establish prima-proof of ownership of copyrights or any interest in copyrights. Thus in conformity with Article 5(2) of the Berne Convention the registration is not compulsory under the law but a work may be got registered maintained in the Copyright office under the control of Registrar of Copyrights. Registrar is also responsible for administration of the whole law having its head office at Karachi and a branch office at Lahore working under administrative control of Ministry of Education. The application for registration and procedure thereof is quite easy and simple and a small amount of registration fee of (Pak Rs.200/- only) about 4 US$) is to be deposited alongwith a copy of the work sought to be registered. After holding an enquiry and exhausting the statutory period of 30 days of receipt of any possible objection to the registration by any interested party, the Registrar may grant or refuse registration. Since the 1992 amendments in law and due to increased copyright awareness the work load of copyright office has increased manifold and at present applications for registration of copyright of various works are being received numbering to about 1800-2000 per year which is about twenty time more than the application previously (prior to 1992 amendments) received. Majority of applications, however relate to artistic works (*e.g.* label designs, drawings, logos, monograms and calligraphies etc.) Literary works, cinematographic and musical works and thereafter respectively. As registration is not compulsory the number of registered works has not been large. However, the number of applications is likely to rise manifold further in coming years with increased awareness of copyright and with establishing/ strengthening of collective administration societies in the private sector.

The law also provides for constitution of a Copyright Board (a soft of quasijudicial special tribunal based at Karachi having its own regulations to run its affairs) which is an appellate authority against any order of the Registrar besides having original jurisdiction, in concurrence with a Court of District Judge while trying a suit, and in certain other copyright matters such as rectification of register of copyright, grant of compulsory licenses in works withheld from public, grant of translations rights and determination of objections relating to fees, charges and royalties concerning the performing right societies. It consists of a Chairman and 5 other members from representatives bodies of the fields concerning the subject of copyright. The Registrar acts as its ex-officio member/Secretary and sits on Board in those cases where his decisions are not challenged. At present there are about 30 rectification applications and appeals pending before it. The work load of the Board is likely to increase further in coming years with the increase in original registration work and with the invocation of its original Jurisdiction by the interested/aggrieved persons.

The law provides adequate remedial measures for the protection of copyright and the economic interest of the authors. In case of any violation and usurpation of the right of an author both civil as well criminal remedies are available under the law. Civil remedies are by way of injunction, damages and accounts, enforceable through a decree of the Court or the Copyright Board. All infringing copies of any work in which copyright subsists and any plates used for the production of such infringing copies shall be deemed to be the property of the owner of copyright. Copyright, being private civil right, legal proceedings have to be initiated by the aggrieved party in the Court of District Judge. However, the case may also be referred to the Copyright Board as an alternative forum to ensure a cheap and speedy remedy as well as officious disposal of the case. The decrees passed by tho Court or the Board are appellable before the High Court. As there had not been much awareness of the existence and availability of rights under copyright law and the protection given to authors, there has not been any significant development in case law on the subject by superior courts, as yet. A provision also exists under the law empowering the Registrar to order a ban on importation of infringing capies of works in concert with the Customs Authorities on being so applied by the aggrieved copyright owner. This provision has been invoked in some cases where infringed copies of the copyrighted works have been seized at customs stage.

As regards criminal remedies the law is now more deterrent. Any unauthorised reproduction and unlawful use/infringement of copyrighted work is considered a serious offence punishable with enhanced fine which extend to one hundred thousand rupees (about 2000 US$) (previously five thousand rupees only) or with enhanced. Imprisonment which may be extended to three years (previously one year only) or with both. The like amount of fine and imprisonment has been provided to cater to some other specific situations of infringement to held curb the menace of piracy more effectively the law has made the offence of piracy cognizable and non-bailable by Police which means an offender now can be arrested even without a warrant from a Magistrate in addition to seizure of pirated material. Besides, the criminal court is further empowered to decree an amount of compensation to be paid to an aggrieved party upto 50% of the fine imposed on the offender in order to make legal proceedings more meaningful. This provision is also perhaps not available in statute of any other developed or developing countries.

The Copyright awareness is gaining momentum in Pakistan and their have been increasing instances of Police raids, arrests and seizures in respect of audio-visual cinematographic and literary works at the instance of their authors/ producers.These have resulted in the arrests and seizures having been made on Video and Book Shops by Police on the complaints of foreign film producers and book authors/publishers. The cases are reported pending disposal in criminal courts. Some cases are also reported pending disposal in civil courts in respect of infringement of copyright. Disposal of cases by the Copyright Board the matters would be brought up before superior courts and thus case law on copyright would be developed in Pakistan. It can, therefore safely be said that the 1992 amendments in Pakistan Copyright Law have been proved useful and encouraging. A lot of healthy response/ compliance is being experienced which is about to grow further with more and more awareness in due course of time. The menace of piracy thus is likely to be curbed to a greater extent, if not eliminated, altogether.

About the amendments made by the latest enactment, *i.e.* Copyright (amendment) Act, 1992 are almost in conformity with the provision of TRIP Agreement, a process has been initiated by the Ministry of Education in concert with WIPO to bring Pakistan Copyright Ordinance, 1952 completely in line with the said Agreement in certain new areas, such as protection of databases, rental rights of authors and performers, the rights of performers and producers of sound recordings, protection of confidential information and border measures etc. The legislative process is expected to be completed during the available transitory period, *viz.* by the end of December,1999. The process of modernizing and computerizing Pakistan Copyright Office is also being undertaken by the Government of Pakistan in cooperation with WIPO. The latest amendments have also been drafted and the final draft has been sent to WIPO, Geneva for their expert comments. The amendments includes important suggestions like specifying the exact amount of penalty in case of infringements instead of open statements such as the fine may extend upto Rs 100,000/-, under this clause some times the fine is only few hundreds only.

Ministry of Science and Technology has drafted a separate legislation for the protection of computer software. A billion Computer Software Act, 99 after passing through all the stages of approvals has been introduced in the National Assembly. It is under consideration by the National Assembly Committee of Science and Technology.

The need for the saperate law has been aroused as sufficient protection under the copyright ordinance Is not available.

THE PATENT SYSTEM

The patent system is the most important form of Industrial Property and also the most dependable method of encouraging scientific and technological research resulting in different Inventions and rewarding them. The precise details of the patent law of a country have to be designed with special care and reference to the economic conditions of the country, the state of Its scientific and technological advances, Its future needs, and other related facts, to effectively minimise, If not, eliminate the possible abuses of a system of patent monopoly. The Patents and Designs Act, 1911 presently in force in Pakistan, being too old does not fulfill the requirements of the country which is a developing one. In addition to the administrative matters as a routine some changes by way of improvement in law are required. The Patent Office is taking all necessary steps to meet the requirements as mentioned above in particular those in view of the decisions reached at in the form of GATT and TRIPS agreements.

THE PATENT OFFICE

Looking through the window of the history it was the late Indian Government which promulgated The Indian Patents and Designs Act, 1911 (Act II of 1911) and also set up the Indian Patent Office on the 2nd January 1912, under section 55 of the Act After Independence, Pakistan inherited the same, and accordingly set up The Patent office at Karachi under section 44 of the Act The Office started functioning. in March 1948 as an independent subordinate office under the Ministry of Industries and now it is an attached department under the same Ministry. The main objectives of the Pakistan Patent Office are:

1. To encourage research and inventions:
2. To disclose new technologies discoveries; and
3. To disseminate technical Information and know-how.

The office fosters the growth of industry by introducing new techniques and know-how. It disseminates patented technology and collaborates with other national as well as International agencies like WIPO and others. The functions of the office are governed by the Patents and Designs Act of 1911. The Controller of Patents and Designs, a statutory officer who is appointed under section 56 of the Act, performs statutory, legal, technical and judicial functions. The Patent Rights itself is a grant from the Government which confers on the grantee for a limited term of 16 years the exclusive privilege of making, selling and using of an "Invention" and also of authorising of others to do so. In fact a patent is granted in exchange for the disclosure of an Invention, it does not endorse the utility claimed by the Inventor In respect of the invention for which It has been granted. A patentable Invention should have following characteristics:

1. It should relate to a manner of manufacture;
2. The manner of manufacture should be novel;
3. It should be the outcome of inventive ingenuity;
4. It should have utility;
5. It should not be contrary to law or morality.

The Act includes elaborate provisions to discourage abuse of the Patent Rights and they are governed by Sections 22 to 25 of the Act. There being a non utilization of an Invention Compulsory license and revocation of a patent can be applied for by any person interested by presenting a petition to the Central Government through the

Patent Office alleging that the demand for a patented article in Pakistan is not being met to an adequate extent and on reasonable terms and praying for the grant of a compulsory license or in the alternative for the revocation of the patent These two provisions available in the Act can be highly beneficial on an Individual as well as collective lever if taken up properly.

PRIORITY PATENT

The basic idea of more and more co-operation on different levels and in different fields resulted in the form of certain reciprocal arrangements for mutual protection of Inventions between Pakistan and some other countries. This protection is possible under section 78-A is a Priority Patent but the same being possible for a limited countries of the world has to be reviewed and it will be done now when the amendments in the Act are being taken up In connection with GATT and TRIPS agreements as already mentioned above. Mutilate co-operation of different nations to the possible extent in possible fields can not be ignored now when the whole world is becoming "Global Village'. In particular due to the highly advanced means of communication In addition to other achievements.

It may be noted as reality that In most developing countries the Industrial Property Offices are unable to function in a manner as expected by the related ones. The main reasons behind this reality are the following in brief:

1. The dominating problem faced by the Patent Office at present is the backlog of pending applications which is caused by the Inter-linked reasons like unfilled vacancies lack of modern equipments or non-utilization thereof due to various reasons.
2. Insufficient office accommodation and storage shortcomings. The present accommodation of the Patent Office is not sufficient to meet the requirements Uhe office demands of the objectives.
3. Insufficient space for library of the Patent Office, which essentially requires space for the storage of documents like Printed Specifications, from the country and abroad, In addition to other valuable books and related literature on scientific, technical and legal topics.
4. Insufficient financial grant to the office which does not enable the office to meet the requirements of the changing circumstances and increase of workload.

DESIGN

The other important form of industrial property is protection of designs or industrial designs. In Pakistan this registration is possible under the Patents and Designs Act 1911 if the feature, shape, configuration pattern or ornament given to the article is new and original. But the registration does not protect the mode or principle of manufacturing the article having such a novel design or shape. A design is registrable for Five years Initially but can be extended for another five years Two times.

15

Development of the Intellectual Property Protection System in Pakistan

S.T.K. Naim

[Chairperson, Pakistan Council for Science and Technology (PCST), Islamabad, Pakistan]

Pakistan has recently upgraded the following IP related legislation/laws in accordance with the international standards and TRIPs agreement. These IP laws are comparable to any developed country of the world.

- Patents Ordinance 2000
- Industrial Design Ordinance 2000
- Layout Design of Integrated Circuits Ordinance 2000.
- Trade Mark Ordinance
- Copy Rights Ordinance

So far there is no codified law for recognition and protection of Geographical Indication. Geographical Indications are extremely important for Pakistan, particularly in reference with the Basmati rice issue. In this context a private law firm, in consultation with Rice Export Association of Pakistan (REAP) and Export Promotion Bureau (EPB) has drafted a new law, which needs to be reviewed and promulgated. The law about the protection of undisclosed information is not significantly important for a country like Pakistan as the law is protected under the common law principles.

The followings are the major issues regarding IPR system in Pakistan:

1. IP offices like Patent Office, Trademark Office, and Copyright Office need to

be strengthened through provision of trained manpower and proper funding.

2. There is also lack of coordination and awareness in the enforcement agencies like police/customs to check the menace of infringement, counterfeiting and piracy. The official of these enforcement agencies needs to be properly trained.
3. There is no proper forum to provide education and training in the IPR field. The law schools in Pakistani universities need to include courses relevant to IPR in their syllabus.
4. Private sector industry managers need to be trained in IPR related matters.

16

Intellectual Property Rights in Saint Lucia

Kimberly Cenac-Phulgence

(Registrar, Registry of Companies and Intellectual Property, Castries, Saint Lucia)

INTELLECTUAL PROPERTY LAWS

Over the last three years, the laws relating to intellectual property have undergone review and in some cases, totally new legislation has been adopted. The major reform of the laws was undertaken between 2000 and 2001 as part of Saint Lucia's attempt to comply with the provisions of the Agreement of Trade Related Aspects of Intellectual Property (TRIPS Agreement). One of the major issues in reviewing the legislation was ascertaining that the laws passed were suitable and workable in the Saint Lucian context. In this regard, the experiences of Australia in trademarks and Singapore in Patents were particularly enlightening.

The intellectual property laws of Saint Lucia consist of seven pieces of legislation. A brief description of these laws follows.

COPYRIGHT

The Copyright Act No. 10 of 1995 replaced the Copyright (St. Lucia) Order, 1965 and the Copyright Act 1956 of the United Kingdom. The main purpose of the Act is provide protection for owners of copyright in literary, dramatic, musical or artistic works, broadcasts, performances by affording then exclusive rights to use their works and preventing use of such protected works without the permission of the copyright owner. The Act also protects computer databases and programmes. The Copyright Act contains certain responsibilities of the Customs Department as part of its compliance with the TRIPS Agreement in providing border measures as part of copyright protection. The Act contains several offences in relation to copyright infringement and gives the police at the rank of superintendent powers of search and seizure where they have reasonable grounds to suspect that an act of infringement is taking place. Of significant note is the fact that registration is not provided for in the Act since copyright protection does not depend on registration. This has proved one of most challenging aspects to explain to the general public who have difficulty in conceptualizing protection without registration.

In the year 2000, the Copyright (Importation Restriction) Regulations Statutory Instrument No. 113 of 2000 were passed to give effect to the provisions relating to the role of Customs in copyright protection affording the copyright owner the opportunity to give notice to the Comptroller of Customs requesting him to treat as prohibited goods copies of the work, film or sound recording for a period not exceeding five years.

The principal Act was amended by the Copyright (Amendment) Act No. 7 of 2000 in the year 2000. This amendment was done primarily to comply with the two Internet Treaties as they are known, the WIPO Copyright Treaty (WCT) and the WIPO Performers and Phonograms Treaty (WPPT). The principal amendments included amendments to the exclusive rights of the copyright owner by adding to the already existing rights, those of communication to the public of the work, rental or public lending of the work, importation of copies of the work among others. This amendment also introduced provisions relating to the set up and operation of a collective society and the Act only permits one such society. The responsibilities and regulatory framework for the society are laid down in the Act. Provision was also made for protection of rights in performances and moral rights of performers.

The Copyright legislation makes provision for all the usual civil remedies, injunctions, damages and accounts. There is also provision for the ordering of seizure of infringing goods, forfeiture of the infringing goods, impounding of copies of the infringing works, order for delivery up of the infringing goods and disposal of infringing goods to be made by the High Court.

LAYOUT-DESIGNS (TOPOGRAPHIES) OF INTEGRATED CIRCUITS

The Layout-Designs (Topographies) of Integrated Circuits Act No. 3 of 2000 and the Layout-Designs (Topographies) of Integrated Circuits Regulations Statutory Instrument No. 49 of 2003 came into force on June 1, 2003. Legislation relating to the protection of layout-designs is new to the intellectual property laws of Saint Lucia and as such there is not much experience under this piece of legislation. Protection is provided under the Act for layout-designs that have not been commercially exploited or have been exploited for not more than two years anywhere in the world. A layout-design to be protected must be original. Protection granted for a term of 10 years from the date of commencement of protection. The effect of protection is to make certain acts unlawful if performed without the authorization of the right holder, for example, reproducing, importing, selling or otherwise distributing for commercial use. The Act provides for offences where a person without authorization performs an unlawful act and provides for a fine and/or imprisonment.

INDUSTRIAL DESIGNS

The Industrial Designs Act No. 2 of 2001 and the accompanying Industrial Designs Regulations Statutory Instrument No. 50 of 2003 entered into force on June 1, 2003. This legislation replaces the provisions of the Commercial Code Cap.244, Title X where they applied to Industrial Designs. This legislation provides protection for industrial designs once they are new. It provides for protection of any composition of lines or colours or any three dimensional form, or any material whether or not associated with lines or colours, where such composition, form or material gives a special appearance to a product of industry or handicraft can serve as a pattern for a product of industry or handicraft, or appeals to and is judged by the eye.

The Act gives the creator of the industrial design exclusive rights and provides that the exploitation of a registered design by persons other than the registered owner shall require the consent of the latter. Exploitation refers to the making, selling, importing or otherwise distributing, for commercial purposes, articles bearing or embodying a design or substantially a copy of the industrial design. The term of protection under the Act is five years and registration can be renewed for two further periods of five years. The owner of a registered design can under the Act institute court proceedings against any person who infringes the registration of an industrial design by exploiting the design without his agreement.

GEOGRAPHICAL INDICATIONS

The protection of geographical indications is another new area which is provided for by the Geographical Indications Act No. 4 of 2000 and the Geographical Indications Regulations Statutory Instrument No. 54 of 2003. These pieces of legislation came into force on June 1, 2003. The Act defines geographical indication as 'an indication, which identifies a good as originating in the territory of a country, or a region or locality in this territory, where a given quality, reputation or other characteristic of the good is essentially attributable to its geographical origin'. The Act provides that only producers carrying on their activity in the geographical area specified shall have the right to use in the course of trade a registered geographical indication, with respect to the products specified in the Register, provided that such products possess the quality, reputation or other characteristics specified in the Register.

The Act makes provision for proceedings to be brought in the High Court to prevent the use of any means in the designation or presentation of a good that indicates or suggests that the good in question originates in a geographical area other than the true place of origin in manner which misleads the public as to the geographical origin of the good, any use which constitutes an act of unfair competition or the use of a geographical indication identifying wines for wines not originating in the place indicated by the geographical indication in question or identifying spirits for spirits not originating in the place indicated by the geographical indication in question, even where the true origin of the goods is indicated or the geographical indication is used in translating or accompanied by expressions such as kind, type, style, imitation or the like.

Additionally, the Act gives the Registrar the power to invalidate the registration of a trademark which contains or consists of a geographical indication with respect to goods not originating in the territory indicated, if use of the indication in the trademark for such goods is of a nature as to mislead the public as to the true place of origin. Similar provisions exist relating to trademarks conflicting with a geographical indication for wines and spirits.

TRADE MARKS

The trademarks legislation in Saint Lucia was previously contained in the Commercial Code Cap.244, Title X. This legislation was repealed by the Trade Marks Act No. 22 of 2001. The Act is accompanied by the Trade Marks Regulations Statutory Instrument No. 17 of 2003. These pieces of legislation came into force on April1, 2003. This new Act made some significant changes to the law relating to trademarks. The term of protection is now ten years from the filing date and not fourteen. Provision is made for the registration of three dimensional shapes, aspects of packaging and shape which could not previously be protected. Another major feature is the aspect relating to the renewal of trademarks where there is no longer any provision for the restoration of marks that have lapsed for failure to renew. The Act also does away with the registration of United Kingdom Trademarks, which existed under the previous legislation.

In keeping with obligations under the TRIPS Agreement, the Act provides for certain border measures somewhat similar to that provided for in the Copyright legislation. It gives the registered trademark owner an opportunity to notify Customs of his registered trademark and file a notice of objection to importation of infringing goods. The Customs authorities are given wide powers of seizure and forfeiture.

The Trade Marks Act 2001 introduced collective, certification and defensive marks which had previously not been provided for. It also makes provision for offences relating to infringement of registered trademarks or falsifying trademarks and contains stiff penalties for these offences. The Trade Marks Regulations provide a comprehensive guide to the procedure relating to the various aspects of the principal Act and seek to provide for all eventualities. The fees relating to trademarks were also revised with the coming of the new legislation and attorneys and their clients are still getting used to these new fees.

ΓROTECTION AGAINST UNFAIR COMPETITION ACT 2000

This is a new piece of legislation introduced to Saint Lucia which is very short and provides for the protection against certain competitive practices that are unfair in the business environment. The legislation because of its recent introduction is still being studied and further development being looked at.

PATENTS

The Patents Act No. 21 of 2001 was passed in April 2001. It repealed the part of the Commercial Code, which dealt with Patents. The old legislation is very outdated and in much need of revision especially in light of the international obligations which Saint Lucia has under various International Agreements. The Act although passed has not entered into force because the accompanying regulations are still being worked on. The Act provides for the filing of national, Paris Convention and international patents whereas previous legislation only provided for the filing of local and United Kingdom patents. It is hoped that by January or April, 2004 the Patents Act and Regulations can enter into force.

17

The Status of Intellectual Property Rights in Tanzania

Y.M. Kohi
(Director General, Tanzania Commission for S&T, Dar-es-Salaam, Tanzania)

The legal history of Tanzania owes to the German and later and in particular the British colonial legacy. At the time of affirming their presence in Tanzania (then Tanganyika) in 1922 and soon thereafter, the British Colonial Office in London introduced English and Indian laws through the famous reception clauses. As such laws of general application found their way into the legal system *of* the new colony; Tanganyika.

The laws that are relevant to intellectual property rights as then incorporated into Tanganyika are:

1. The Patent Registration Ordinance, Chapter 217 of 1931.
2. The Trade Marks Registration Ordinance, 1936, repealed and replaced by the Trade Marks Ordinance, Chapter 394 of 1957.
3. United Kingdom Designs (Protection) Ordinance, Chapter 219 of 1936, automatically extending privileges and rights of UK regulations to Tanganyika without further procedures.

All these laws *de facto* and *de jure* extended the UK territorial jurisdiction to Tanganyika.

ENACTMENT OF NEW IPR LAWS

After independence in 1961 the intellectual property laws were renewed and currently consist of the following:

1. The Copyright Act, 1966.

2. The Trade and Service Marks Act, 1986.
3. The Patent Act 1987, became operational on 1/9/1994.
4. United Kingdom Designs (Protection) Ordonance Chapter 219 of 1936 is still in force in Tanzania although the original UK Patent and Design Act 1907-1932 has since been repealed. This Act is under review in Tanzania.
5. The fair Practices Act. 1994, This was enacted in order to encourage competition in the economy by prohibiting restrictive trade practices regulating monopolies, concentration of economic power and prices, to protect consumer and to provide for other related matters.

RATIFICATION OF INTERNATIONAL TREATIES/ AGREEMENTS ON IPR

1. The Paris Convention for the Protection of Industrial Property, 1883, ratified on 16 June 1963.
2. The Convention establishing WIPO, 1967, ratified on 30 December 1983.
3. The BERNE Convention, 1886, ratified on 25 July 1994.
4. World Trade Organisation/Trade Related Intellectual Property Rights (WTO/TRIPS) Agreement, ratified on 15 April 1994.
5. African Regional Intellectual Rights Organisation, ARIRO, 1976, ratified on 9 December 1976. Within the African continent, Tanzania is therefore a Party to and has ratified the ARIRO Agreement of 1976, and is a signatory to both the Harare Protocol for Protection of Patents and Industrial Designs and the Bangul Protocol for the Protection of Trade Marks. Since Tanzania is also a party to the World Trade Organisation (WTO) and the Trade Related Intellectual Property Rights *(TRIPS)* Agreement then by the year 2005 Tanzania will be expected to have complied with the provisions of the TRIPS Agreement that came into force with the establishment of the World Trade Organisation (WTO) on 1/1/1995. The ten year grace period for developing countries to provide for product protection under the TRIPS provisions dates from the establishment of the WTO.

PROPOSED AND *IN SITU* LEGISLATION

1. The Patent Act, 1987, did not become operational until 1/9/1994, over a decade since the draft concept eventually evolved into a bill and enacted by Parliament. The Act therefore is in dire need of amendment to bring it in line with the newer global legislations in *pari materia.* The Uganda Patent Act 1991, operational since 1993, is a relevant example. It has provisions for plant and animal vareties and biological processes for the production of plants or animals, among others.
2. With support from WIPO, a suitable and current industrial design law is being drafted to repeal and replace the over a half a century old British law.
3. Plant Breeders Rights: In consultation with our Ministry of Agriculture and Cooperatives a process has been initiated that will lead to the enactment

of a law for the recognition and protection of plant breeders rights. The plant breeders rights under the existing international agreement have immense dimensions and implications for third world countries which are bound to internalize international model laws or develop *sui generis* systems which must in some way not contradict trade liberalisation under WTO/ TRIPS Agreements, especially as provided for under Article 27(3) (b) of the TRIPS Agreement. This article in essence obliges parties to the TRIPS Agreement fronde for the protection of plant vareties either by patents or by a specific law or a combination of both. The impetus of the Union for the Protection of New Plant Vaneties (UPOV) will need to be considered by Tanzania as she prepares towards the enactment of the plant breeders rights.

CONCLUSION

The trend for the protection of knowledge through statutory provisions established through the concept and legal realism of intellectual property rights is now conspicuously unstoppable. In issue is the extent to which this process should extend. Should this include plant and animal vareties (?) or biological process for the production of plants and/or animals. It is a question of paramount importance as to how best developing countries in particular can protect their national interests yet comply and conform to their obligations in WTO. That is currently in issue and Tanzania wishes to benefit from the position being adopted by the third world countries in the South. This is one such forum and the output of this workshop will be an important input into our ongoing process in view of the legally global realism.

18

INTELLECTUAL PROPERTY RIGHTS IN TRINIDAD AND TOBAGO

Richard Aching

(Chief Technical Examiner, Intellectual Property Office, Ministry of Legal Affairs, Port of Spain, Republic of Trinidad and Tobago)

INTELLECTUAL PROPERTY LEGISLATION: THE LEGAL FRAMEWORK

Existing Legislation

The Intellectual Property Office, Trinidad and Tobago was created on the 1st December, 1997 (Section 3 of the Patents Act, 1996) and it is situated at 72 – 74 South Quay, Port of Spain.

The Intellectual Property Laws in force are as follows:

1. The Patents Act, 1996 (Act No. 21 of 1996), The Patent Validation Act, 1999 (Act No. 5 of 1999), The Miscellaneous Amendments Act, 2000 (No. 18 of 2000), The Patents Amendment Act, 2000 (Act No. 54 of 2000),
2. The Trade Mark Act (Chapter 82:81) and Amendment (Act No. 17 of 1994, No. 25 of 1996, No. 31 of 1997)
3. The Geographical Indications Act, 1996 (Act No. 20 of 1996)
4. The Industrial Designs Act, 1996 (Act No. 18 of 1996)
5. The Layout-Designs (Topographies) of Integrated Circuits Act, 1996 (Act No. 19 of 1996)
6. The Protection of New Plant Varieties Act, 1997 (Act No. 7 of 1997)
7. The Copyright Act, 1997 (Act No. 8 of 1997)

8. The Protection Against Unfair Competition Act, 1996 (Act No. 27 of 1996)
9. The Miscellaneous Amendments Act, 2000 (Act No. 18 of 2000)

The associated Intellectual Property Rules and Regulations are as follows:

1. The Patents Rules, 1996
2. The Trade Mark Rules (Chapter 82:81), Trademark Amendment Rules (Act No. 45 of 1979), Trademark Amendment Rules (Act No. 17 of 1994) and Trademark Amendment Rules 1997 (Act No. 31 of 1997)
3. The Geographical Indications Regulations, 1996
4. The Industrial Designs Rules, 1996
5. The Layout-Designs (Topographies) of Integrated Circuits Rules, 1996
6. The Protection of New Plant Varieties Regulations, 2000
7. The Copyright (Customs) Regulations, 2000

While all of the above modes of protection are available, applications have only been filed for trademarks, patents, industrial designs and utility certificates in decreasing order.

List of Draft Laws and Bills, Still Under Consideration, for the Modification of Existing Legislation in Intellectual Property

1. Copyright Amendment Bill, 2003
2. Trademark Amendment Bill, 2003
3. Patent Amendment Bill, 2000.

Compliance of Existing Legislation with the Agreement on Trade-Related Aspects of Intellectual Property Rights (TRIPs)

Trinidad and Tobago's intellectual property legislation successfully underwent legislative review by the TRIPs Council on June 2000. The question and answer process occurred between June 6, 2000 and August 1, 2000. A list of the questions posed by World Trade Organization (WTO) members and answers returned by Trinidad and Tobago are contained in the following WTO documents:

WTO Document Number	*Title*	*Date*
1. IP/C/W/179	Review of Legislation: Responses from Trinidad and Tobago to Questions Posed by Japan	6 June 2000
2. IP/C/W/174	Review of legislation: Questions posed by the United States	7 June 2000
3. IP/N/6/TTO/1	Checklist of Issues on Enforcement: Responses from Trinidad And Tobago	13 April 2000
4. IP/C/W/184	Review of Legislation: Questions Posed by Canada	20 June 2000
5. IP/C/W/179/Add.1	Review of Legislation: Responses from Trinidad and Tobago to Questions Posed by the European Communities and their member States and the United States Addendum	23 June 2000

WTO Document Number	*Title*	*Date*
6. IP/Q/TTO/1, IP/Q2/TTO/1, IP/Q3/TTO/1, IP/Q4/TTO/1	Review of legislation: Trinidad and Tobago	1 August 2000

List of Bilateral and Multilateral Agreements, Regional and Sub-regional Initiatives in the Filed of Intellectual Property to which Trinidad and Tobago is a Party [accession date]

1. The Paris Convention for the Protection of Industrial Property (1883). [1st August 1964]
2. The Locarno Agreement establishing an International Classification for Industrial Designs (1968). [20th March 1996]
3. The Berne Convention for the Protection of Literary and Artistic Works (1886). [16th August 1988]
4. The Patent Cooperation Treaty (PCT) (1970). [10th March 1994]
5. The Geneva Convention for the Protection of Producers of Phonograms against Unauthorized Duplication of their Phonograms (1971). [1st October 1988]
6. The Strasbourg Agreement concerning the International Patent Classification (1971). [20th December 1996]
7. The Budapest Treaty of the International Recognition of the Deposit of Micro organisms for the Purposes of Patent Procedure (1977). [10th March 1994]
8. The Nice Agreement concerning the International Classification of Goods and Services for the Purposes of the Registration of marks (1957). [20th March 1996]
9. Vienna Agreement establishing an International Classification of the Figurative Elements of Marks (1973). [20th March 1996]
10. The Brussels Convention Relating to the Distribution of Programme Carrying Signals Transmitted By Satellite (1974). [1st November 1996]
11. Trademark Law Treaty (TLT) (1994). [16th April 1998]
12. Union for the Protection of New Plant Varieties (UPOV). [30th January 1998]
13. Convention Establishing the World Intellectual Property Organization (1967). [16th August 1998]
14. The Universal Copyright Convention as revised in Paris (1971). [19th August 1998]
15. Memorandum of Understanding between the Republic of Trinidad and Tobago and the United States of America concerning Protection of Intellectual Property (1994). [26th September 1994]

16. The Agreement on the Trade Related Aspects of Intellectual Property Rights (1995). [1st March 1995]

NOTES

The Cabinet of the Government of the Republic of Trinidad has approved accession to the World Intellectual Property Organization Copyright Treaty (WCT) and the World Intellectual Property Organization Performances and Phonograms Treaty (WPPT). Accession, however, is pending because certain amendments to our Copyright Act, 1997 are necessary in order for us to comply with the WIPO Performances and Phonograms Treaty and the WIPO Copyright Treaty. The Bill is presently with the Chief Parliamentary Counsel and will soon be placed on the Law Revision Commission's Agenda before being taken to Parliament. The draft Bill was also forwarded to WIPO for comments.

International, Regional and Bilateral Treaties, Conventions and Agreements not under the purview of the Ministry of Legal Affairs with an Intellectual Property Component:

There are a number of International, Regional and Bilateral Conventions, Agreements and Treaties that are not under the purview of the Ministry of Legal Affairs, Intellectual Property Office that contain a significant Intellectual Property Component these are:

1. The Trade and Economic Cooperation Agreement between the Caribbean Community (CARICOM) and the Government of the Republic of Cuba
2. The Trade and Economic Cooperation Agreement between the Caribbean Community (CARICOM) and the Government of Costa Rica
3. The Trade and Economic Cooperation Agreement between the Caribbean Community (CARICOM) and the Government of the Dominican Republic

There are also a number of similar type agreements that are under consideration and these are:

1. The Agreement on the Free Trade Areas of the Americas
2. The Free Trade Agreement between the Republic of Trinidad and Tobago and the United States of Mexico
3. The Agreement between the Government of the Republic of Trinidad and Tobago and the Government of the Republic of Indonesia

World Intellectual Property Organization Treaties under consideration:

1. The Patent Law Treaty
2. An International Instrument for folklore, Traditional Knowledge and access to Genetic Resources

Types of Classification Used in the Field of Industrial Property (national, international and statutory)

Trinidad and Tobago is party to 4 international classification treaties that are applied in classifying industrial property applications for registration. These treaties in the fields of patents, industrial designs and trademarks are as follows [*accession date*]:

1. The Strasbourg The Strasbourg Agreement concerning the International Patent Classification (1971). [20th December 1996]
2. The Locarno Agreement establishing an International Classification for Industrial Designs (1968). [20th March 1996]
3. The Nice Agreement concerning the International Classification of Goods and Services for the Purposes of the Registration of marks (1957). *[20th March 1996]*
4. Vienna Agreement establishing an International Classification of the Figurative Elements of Marks (1973). *[20th March 1996]*

Presently, Trinidad and Tobago is using the latest editions of these classification treaties except for the Nice Classification. The latest edition of the Nice Classification is the Eighth Edition. The Seventh Edition is still being used and will continue to be used until the necessary amendment is made to the Trademark Rules. This revision is at the moment with the Chief Parliamentary Counsel of the Ministry of the Attorney General. In the revision of our trademark law, a provision will be added to allow for the use of the latest amendments to the classification as soon as changes are agreed to by the member states of WIPO.

INTELLECTUAL PROPERTY ADMINISTRATION

Competent National Authority

The Intellectual Property Office, Ministry of Legal Affairs, 3rd Floor Registration House, 72-74 South Quay, Port of Spain, Trinidad and Tobago. The Trinidad and Tobago IPO is responsible for the examination and grant of industrial property rights for trademarks, patents, utility certificates, industrial designs, layout designs (topographies) of integrated circuits and new plant varieties. The TTIPO also serves as a Designated Office, Elected Office and Receiving Office for patent applications filed under the Patent Cooperation Treaty (PCT).

Mandate and Functions

Vision Statement

The Intellectual Property Office is striving to become a dynamic and progressive organization which stimulates creative effort in industry and commerce in Trinidad and Tobago. The Office constantly seeks to develop and promote appropriate legislation for the protection of all forms of intellectual effort internationally. It is staffed by dedicated, well-trained people on a workplace conducive to efficiency and innovation. It is our vision to see the Office become a full self-financing organization which makes an effective financial contribution to the Government of Trinidad and Tobago.

Mission Statement

To stimulate research and creativity within the Republic of Trinidad and Tobago by providing intellectual property rights and the legal means for their protection and encouraging the public disclosure and the effective use of accurate information on creative effort thereby enhancing the competitiveness and contributing to the economic and social development of the people of Trinidad and Tobago.

Responsibilities of the Office

1. The substantive examination and grant of Intellectual Property Rights.
2. The determination of Opposition Hearings.
3. Making Intellectual Property information available to the public.
4. Receipt of international-applications under the Patent Cooperation Treaty (PCT).
5. Advise the Government on Intellectual Property matters, *e.g.* for negotiation in the trade agreements.
6. The conduct of public awareness activities to the public, inclusive of schools and institutions of higher learning.
7. Promotion of inventiveness among the citizens of Trinidad and Tobago.
8. Making Patent Technical Information available to inventors, researchers, etc.
9. Participation in the development of International Treaties in the area of Intellectual Property; and
10. Participation in the development of International Instruments dealing with new and evolving areas of Intellectual Property

Staff and Training Requirements 2004

Training will be pursued under the following headings

1. On the Job
2. Study Visits
3. Expert Missions
4. Through the Bureau for Latin America and the Caribbean and the WIPO Academy

On the Job

All members of staff participate in, on the job training. We have taken advantage of the WIPO Distance Learning Introductory Course. Staff will participate in the Advanced Courses.

Study Visits

With respect to Study Visits for 2003/2004 the following requests will be made:

1. Study visit of Patent Examiner to the UK Patent Office – Examinations. (Request already made to the Latin American and Caribbean Bureau) Recommendation arising out of Mr. Barford's Mission in 2003;

2. Study visit of Technical Information Specialist are: Development of Library Services either to the Franklin Pierce Law Center or another appropriate office. Request made in 2003. Will be renewed in 2004; and
3. Classification – Trademark Examiner I to WIPO.

Expert Missions

1. The Hague Agreement (for staff and Intellectual Property Agents);
2. WIPO Expert to train new staff (Technicians, Assistant Controller);
3. Trademark Classification (for Agents);
4. Workshop for Clerks and Agents – pre filing of Patents (member of staff to conduct training);
5. General training in intellectual property for staff. (Experts from Trinidad and Tobago and staff to do presentations) once a month on any Intellectual Property issue.

WIPO Fellowship Award Scheme– (To pursue varying levels)

1. Technical Information Specialist in the area of Patent Information Services
2. Copyright and Related Rights for the Legal Officer
3. Trademark Administration for the Trademark Examiner II
4. Interregional Intermediate Seminar on Industrial Property for the Assistant Trademark Examiner
5. WIPO Academy for the Chief Technical Examiner in the Session for Senior Government officials.

Technical Infrastructure

The Intellectual Property Office currently has a LAN consisting of 40 workstations and 5 servers. The Intellectual Property Office hosts its own website at www.ipo.gov.tt internally and is serviced via a 128KB leased circuit. While content on the website is fairly static "brochureware", it is the intention to upgrade the site to be able to publish the databases online allowing users to query the industrial property databases and also file applications online. The same leased circuit also grants Internet access to officers allowing use of communications and access to several online industrial property databases hoste by larger offices.

Databases in the Field of Trademarks, Patents, Industrial Designs and Other Industrial Property Rights

With the assistance of WIPO, the Intellectual Property Office has been able to fully implement the Intellectual Property Rights Administration System (IPRAS) for both the trademarks and patents modules. This system was developed by WIPO for the IP offices of the Caribbean. By mid November 2003 the IPO anticipates that attorneys and agents will be able to visit the Office and conduct their trademark searches interactively on the database.

Currently the trademark module is used to administer all stages of the process from application to registration (including renewals). Installation of the patents module took place in the second quarter of 2003 and the Office is in the process of verifying the data that was captured. It is projected that by January 2004 the information in the database will be accurate and complete and available for public searching.

Promotion of Intellectual Property at the National Level

The Promotion of Intellectual Property is a continuous activity with specific long-term goals/objectives. These goals are on the one hand for users to respect the efforts of creators of Intellectual Property by refraining from acts that infringe on the creators' right to receive economic reward and to be associated with their works. On the other hand it is for the creators to use the Intellectual Property System not only to protect their works but to disclose their creations which will further inspire innovative effort to create new or improve upon existing works. It is this innovative effort that fuels a knowledge based society and economy.

The corporate and individual populations of Trinidad and Tobago are divided into segments of similar characteristics, fields of endeavour and the nature of their demand or influence on the Intellectual Property System. Examples of these groups are Students at primary, secondary and tertiary level educational institutions, teachers/lecturers of same, small and medium sized enterprises, policymakers and senior technocrats, especially within the Ministries responsible for Education, Trade, Foreign Affairs, Science and Technology, Health, Culture and Finance, creators of Intellectual Property and more especially their associated non-governmental organisations, for example the Inventors Organisations, Authors Organisations and any like organizations, Copyright Collective Management Organisations, Business Organisations, like the Chambers of Commerce, Manufacturers Associations and the of course the general public. Another Public Education Strategy of the Intellectual Property Office is to focus deliberate efforts on those groups from which the greatest long-term benefit will result; however there are some activities that are applicable to a wide cross section of these groups.

These cross segment activities include the Intellectual Property Library which is open to all members of the public and which contains over 6,000,000 patents from around the world in DVD-ROMS or CD-ROMS. The Library also provides access to online patent databases which includes countries as diverse as the United States of America, Europe, Peoples Republic of China and Republic of Korea.

The Intellectual Property Office has created and maintains a website to leverage the resources of the Office so that information will be available at any time and accessible from any place. The website contains information on the Intellectual Property related International Treaties and Agreements, the Intellectual Property Laws of Trinidad and Tobago, Information in Question and Answer format on Patents, Industrial Designs, Trademarks, Copyright and Related Rights, Protection for the Layout Designs of Integrated Circuits, New Plant Variety Protection and Geographical Indications as well as an Introduction to Intellectual Property and an Intellectual Property Tree. The Website also contains a document library, which in turn contains documents from various Seminar and Workshops held on Intellectual Property. The website also facilitates discussion on topical issues. One of the Strategies used to encourage use of and respect for Intellectual Property and the Intellectual Property System is to make Intellectual Property Information, especially Patent Information, available for research. In the near future persons will be able to conduct basic searches of the Patent and Trademark databases online.

All Intellectual Property Offices around the world celebrate World Intellectual Property Day on the 26th April, or the closest working day to it, each year. This celebration is used as a focal point for other Intellectual Property related activities. The key activity is an exhibition which is open to all.

The Intellectual Property Office has produced and distributed publications on each area of Intellectual Property Patents, Industrial Designs, Trademarks, Copyright and Related Rights, Protection for the Layout Designs of Integrated Circuits, New Plant Variety Protection and Geographical Indications as well as an Introduction to Intellectual Property, an Intellectual Property Tree and a brochure on Unfair Competition widely.

Another Public Education Strategy of the Intellectual Property Office is to focus deliberate efforts on those groups from which the greatest long term benefit will result. The segment specific activities are Seminars, Workshops designed for specific target groups, more specifically, seminars on Intellectual Property for Small and Medium Sized Enterprises and Journalists. Also there were Workshops held on Patent Claim Drafting for Patent Agents and Attorneys and on Geographical Indications for prospective users of Geographic Indications in Trinidad and Tobago.

As mentioned in paragraph 2, one of the most critical areas for focus is education. A proposal has been made to the Ministry of Education to introduce Intellectual Property in the Schools Curriculum. To complement the introduction of Intellectual Property into the Schools Curriculum a programme for teaching the Teachers on the Intellectual Property has been approved and will be executed. One of our most important focused activities is the ongoing School Lecture series where lectures are given at Secondary and University levels to 3rd, 4th, 5th and 6th Form students to introduce Intellectual Property and demonstrate how respecting the creators rights is necessary. There is also a Visiting lecture programme to business, creator and user organizations on the Business implications of Intellectual Property, managing Intellectual Property, and Patent Information for Research purposes. A colloquium for Judges on Intellectual Property is scheduled for the first quarter of 2004 to strengthen the capacity of the Judiciary in this regard will be complimented by a workshop on enforcement for enforcement officers such as the Director of Public Prosecutions Department, Customs and Police. Proposals have been made to the Hugh Wooding Law School and the Faculty of Law of the University of the West Indies to include Intellectual Property Law in their respective syllabi.

The electronic and print media are frequently used to discuss topical issues as they arise. The Office also promotes the use of appropriate WIPO produced material to assist in the Public Education effort. The WIPO CD-Rom "At Home with Inventions" and WIPO-produced Comics on Patents, Trademarks and Copyright were distributed to all Secondary Schools in Trinidad and Tobago to create awareness of Intellectual Property. Also a WIPO CD-ROM Resource on Intellectual Property for Small and Medium Enterprises was distributed to SME's in Trinidad and Tobago.

The Office promotes the use of the WIPO Distance Learning Programme DL 101 and Advanced Distance Learning Modules for those individuals seeking a deeper understanding of Intellectual Property. The Intellectual Property Office is also in the process of modifying publications of WIPO, with their permission, such as the WIPO SME publication making a trademark.

INDUSTRIAL PROPERTY STATISTICS

Applications

Period	*Origin*	*Patents*	*Trademarkes*	*Industrial Desings*	*Utility Certificates*
2001	Resident	4	1116	5	1
	Non-resident	235		1	1
2002	Resident	2	1106	1	2
	Non-resident	221		1	2
2003(to	Resident	0	749	1	1
8/10/03)	Non-resident	169		6	1
TOTAL*		**631**	**2971**	**15**	**8**

Grants

Period	*Origin*	*Patents*	*Trademarkes*	*Industrial Desings*	*Utility Certificates*
2001	Resident	0	318	0	0
	Non-resident	3	1237	0	0
2002	Resident	0	189	8	0
	Non-resident	17	917	10	0
2003 (to	Resident	0	49	1	4
8/10/03)	Non-resident	100	307	5	0
TOTAL*		**120**	**3017**	**24**	**4**

*Total for 2001 to 8/10/2003

19

STATE POLICY AND LEGISLATION ON INTELLECTUAL PROPERTY IN UKRAINE

Constantine V. Subbotin

(Embassy of Ukraine, New Delhi, India)

INTRODUCTION

Ukrainian intellectual property legislation is one of the most comprehensively regulated branches of Ukrainian legislation nowadays. It affords protection, inter alia, to copyright and neighboring rights, inventions, utility models, industrial designs, trademarks and service marks, appellations of origin, layouts of integrated circuits, etc.

Ukrainian intellectual property legislation develops in line with applicable international standards and has the tendency for its approximation with the laws of the European Union. Specifically, the Partnership and Cooperation Agreement, entered into by and between the European Union (the EU) and Ukraine, provides that Ukraine will implement certain EU directives in the area of intellectual property and will accede to a number of international agreements governing intellectual property issues.

Ukraine is a party to the Berne Convention, Paris Convention, Madrid Agreement, Patent Cooperation Treaty and numerous other international multi-or bilateral agreements on the protection of intellectual property. Ukraine has also declared its intention to join the World Trade organization (the WTO) in the near future and, thus, to subject itself to the requirements of the TRIPs Agreement.

COPYRIGHT

Protection of Rights in Software

In Ukraine, software is protected under the Law of Ukraine on the "Protection of Copyright and Related Rights", as a literary work of authorship. Copyright protection extends both to operational systems and applications, expressed in source and/or object codes, including the preparatory materials and the audiovisual designs of the programs.

For purposes of the Copyright Law, "software" is defined as a selection of instructions, expressed in words, numbers, codes, schemes, symbols, or any other means of expression, comprehendible by a computer.

Copying of a computer program without charge is permitted if one copy is made (or adaptation is made) by the lawful user of the computer program, for the use of the computer program on a particular computer, or for archival purposes (to serve as a replacement of a lawfully acquired copy in a case of loss or damage).

The free reverse engineering of a computer program is permitted for the reproduction of the program's code and for the translation of its form with the view of receiving the information necessary for the attainment of the compatibility of an independently created computer program with other computer programs, provided that the following conditions are met:

- The act of reverse engineering is carried out by the lawful owner of a copy of the computer program or by a person duly authorized by such lawful owner;
- The information necessary for the attainment of such compatibility is not known to the person specified in (1) prior to the act of reverse engineering; and
- The reverse engineering is limited only to those elements of the computer program, which are necessary for the attainment of the compatibility.

Ukrainian legislation provides for a distinction between "moral" and "economic" rights embedded in copyright. The Copyright Law provides that moral rights shall always remain with the natural person who is the author of a given work. Economic rights in the work may belong to the same person or to a third one. In particular, the "exclusive property rights" in a copyrighted work may belong to such person's employer or another party, which hired the author to create the particular copyrighted work. It is important to understand that under the Copyright Law economic rights of third parties in the works-for-hire may only take the form of exclusive property rights.

Protection of Rights in Databases

Rights in databases are also protected under the Copyright Law. Pursuant to the Copyright Law, "databases" are defined as collections of works, data or any other independent information, selected and arranged as a result of creative work, integral parts of which could be accessed by means of special search engines.

Any database is afforded copyright protection if it is the result of creative work on the selection and assembling of its contents, subject to the condition that no violation of any copyright in the constituent works took place during the creation of the database.

Protection of Information in Automated Databases

The protection of information in automated databases is subject to the Law of Ukraine on the "Protection of Information in Automated Databases" dated 5 July 1994 (the Automated Databases Law). The Automated Databases Law establishes principles for the regulation of relations between the parties involved in the processing of information in automated databases and the use of such information by third parties. It also provides for the protection of the rights of the owners of the information processed in automated databases.

The Automated Databases Law defines "automated databases" as systems designed for the automated processing of data Information in automated databases is subject to protection regardless of the means of expression of the information.

The Automated Databases Law requires that access to the information in the automated databases must be subject to rules established by the owner of the processed information or by a person duly authorized by the owner. Furthermore, the Automated Database Law mandates that a person at fault for the loss or the disclosure of information from an automated database system must be required to reimburse the damages inflicted upon an interested party as a result of such loss or disclosure. However, the owner of an automated database system is not liable for any damage inflicted on the owner of the information processed in the automated database system, unless the damage results from a breach of the rules on the protection of the information established by the owner of such information.

Industrial Property

Patents for Inventions and Utility Models

Protection for patents for inventions and utility models in Ukraine is granted in accordance with the Law of Ukraine on the "Protection of Rights in Inventions and Utility Models" dated 15 December 1993 (the Inventions Law).

Ukraine follows the principle of universal novelty in granting patents. This means that an invention must be absolutely new worldwide within the relevant technological or scientific area. Inventions are required to meet each of the following requirements, in order to be granted patent protection:

- Novelty;
- Non-obviousness; and
- Utility.

The Inventions Law provides for a twelve month grace period for any public disclosure of information about an invention by the inventor or by any third person, who directly or indirectly obtained such information from the inventor.

A patent may be issued for an invention in the name of the inventor, his/her employer, or his/her legal successors. As a general rule, an inventor is entitled to patent his/her own invention unless the Inventions Law provides otherwise. In all cases, the inventor is entitled to retain indefinitely the rights of authorship in his/her invention.

An invention "made for hire" should be patented in the name of the employer to the extent that such invention is made within the scope of the employee's employment obligations, pursuant to the direct instructions of the employer, or with the use of the expertise, know-how, secrets, and/or equipment of the employer. Employers and employees are authorized to provide for different conditions for the patenting of inventions in the employment agreements concluded by them.

Patents are granted to inventions for 20 years from the priority date. Patents for inventions related to medicine and adjacent areas may be further extended for a maximum period of 5 years. The term of patent validity is conditioned upon the payment of annual maintenance fees.

The Inventions Law provides for the concept of a declaratory patent for the protection of inventions and utility models. Only declaratory patents may protect utility models, while either a declaratory or a regular patent may be granted for an invention. Declaratory patents for inventions are issued for a term of 6 years and those for utility models for a term of 10 years.

Declaratory patents for inventions are granted on the basis of only a formal examination, to the extent provided that the invention meets the standard of local novelty. Any declaratory patent for an invention may be converted into a regular patent at the request of the applicant or a third person, provided that a demand for a substantive examination of the invention is filed within three years after the initial application date.

Ukraine is a party to a number of international conventions facilitating filing for patent protection of inventions, among them the Paris Convention, the Patent Cooperation Treaty, the new Agreement on Patent Legislation etc.

Protection of Trademarks

Protection for trademarks in Ukraine is granted in accordance with the Law of Ukraine on the "Protection of Rights in Trademarks and Service marks" dated 15 December 1993 (the Trademark Law).

The current Ukrainian legislation affords protection to only two types of trademarks and service marks:

- Marks registered in Ukraine pursuant to the Trademark Law; and
- Trademarks and trade names, which are not registered in Ukraine, but which enjoy protection pursuant to the international agreements; to which Ukraine is a party (so called "international trademark registrations").

Trademarks pending registration enjoy temporary protection until the relevant registration certificates are granted. Ukraine grants trademark protection for a term of ten years from the filing date. At the request of the owner of the mark, and upon the payment of the required extension fee, trademark registrations may be extended an indefinite number of times for additional ten-year periods.

As a member of the Madrid Union, Ukraine honors international trademark registrations extended to the territory of Ukraine, both under the Madrid Agreement and under the Madrid Protocol.

Protection of Rights in Layouts of Integrated Circuits (Mask Works)

In Ukraine, rights in layouts of integrated circuits are protected under the Law of Ukraine on the "Protection of Rights in the Layout Design of Integrated Circuits", dated 5 November 1997 (the Layout Design Law).

The Layout Design Law defines a "layout of integrated circuits" (the Layout Design) as a three-dimensional pattern of the aggregate of the integrated circuit's elements fixed in a tangible medium.

Rights in a Layout Design arise upon the registration of the Layout Design with the patent and trademark authority of Ukraine. The originality of the Layout Design is a prerequisite for its registration.

A Layout Design is presumed to be original if (1) it is not created by means of the direct reproduction of another Layout Design; (2) it was not known in the field of microelectronics prior to the date of the application for its registration or prior to the date of its first use; and (3) it is characterized by new qualities, differentiating it from other Layout Designs. Any Layout Design submitted for registration is presumed to be original unless sufficient evidence to the contrary is provided.

The rights in a Layout Design include:

- The right to use the Layout Design;
- The right to preclude other parties from using the Layout Design
- The right to assign rights in the Layout Design to another person; and
- The right to license the use of the Layout Design to another person.

An assignment of rights in, and a license of the use of, a Layout Design are valid with respect to third parties only if they are registered with the patent and trademark authority of Ukraine. Rights in a Layout Design are evidenced by a certificate of registration of the Layout Design issued by the patent and trademark authority of Ukraine. This certificate is valid for 10 years starting from the date of the application for the registration of the Layout Design, or from the date of its first use, provided that the application for the registration of the Layout Design was filed not later than two years after the date of its first use.

As a general rule, the author of a Layout Design is entitled to register it. However, in the event that a Layout Design is created by the author in connection with the performance of the author's employment duties and/or under a specific assignment from the author's employer, then the right to register the Layout Design vests with the employer, unless the employment agreement provides otherwise. Irrespective of the above, the author retains the right of authorship, which right remains inalienable.

TAXATION

The general principles of the Ukrainian tax system, as well as the types of taxes and duties (mandatory payments) which may be levied in Ukraine, are defined in the Law on the "Taxation System" (the Tax System Law). The Tax System Law stipulates that tax rates, tax exemptions, and procedures and mechanisms for tax assessments and payments may not be introduced or changed by legislative acts other than special tax laws. In addition, any changes or amendments with regard to the determination of tax rates, tax exemptions, and procedures and mechanisms for their assessment and payment may be introduced into the tax legislation not less than 6 months before the beginning of the new budget year, and should take effect at the beginning of the new budget year.

The Tax System Law provides for certain categories of taxes, which may be levied in Ukraine. There are two categories of taxes in Ukraine: national and local. National taxes and duties are established by Verkhovna Rada of Ukraine and are levied on the nation-wide basis. Local taxes and duties (mandatory payments), and the mechanisms and procedures for their assessment and payment, are established by local village or city councils in accordance with, and within the maximum rates established by, the laws of Ukraine.

With the adoption of the Law of Ukraine on the "Procedure for the Settlement of Obligations of Taxpayers to the Budgets and the State Purposive Funds", there were established the uniform rules for, inter alia, filing tax returns and settlement of tax liabilities, the statutory period of limitation of three years for payment of tax liabilities, rates and procedure for calculating penalty interest for the late tax payment and penalties for violation of tax rules, the administrative procedure for appealing the assessment of tax deficiencies.

Corporate income tax (CIT) and value-added tax (VAT) are the principal national taxes that affect business activities of legal entities in Ukraine.

Corporate Income Tax

The law of Ukraine on the "Taxation of Profits of Enterprises", as amended (the CIT Law), is the principal law governing the income tax liabilities of corporate taxpayers in Ukraine. The CIT Law was completely amended and restated on 22 May 1997, and became effective on 1 July 1997.

The following persons are subject to CIT:

- Resident business entities, state, public and other types of enterprises, institutions, and organizations, which generate profits from their activity, both within and outside of the territory of Ukraine;
- Non-resident physical persons and legal entities, which derive profits from Ukrainian sources, with the exception of diplomatic establishments and other organizations enjoying immunity from taxation;
- Branches, divisions, and other separate units of taxpayers identified above, which are not legal entities and which are located in a territorial community other than the territorial community of such taxpayer; and

- Permanent establishments of non-residents, which derive profits from Ukrainian sources or which act as agents (*i.e.* representatives) for such non-residents.

The CIT Law has established a basic corporate tax rate of 30%. The corporate profits tax is levied on "profits" which are considered to be equal to the adjusted gross income of the taxpayer in any given reporting period minus all allowable expenses and depreciation. "Gross income" is defined as the aggregate revenues obtained by an enterprise in monetary, in kind, or non-material forms from all of its activities carried out in Ukraine and abroad during the reporting period.

Under the CIT Law, all reasonable business expenses of the corporate taxpayer are allowed as deductions, unless they are expressly limited or prohibited by law. Such limited and prohibited deductions include, inter alia:

- Interest payments on a loan by the borrower, in which the share of the foreign shareholder is 50% or more, and which is making interest payments in favor of another taxpayer, in which the share of a foreign shareholder is 50% or more – the allowed deduction is limited to 50% of the taxable income in the reporting period, in which the corporate taxpayer pays the interest, pus any income obtained in the form of interest;
- Payments to offshore territories, a list of which is made public annually be the Cabinet of Ministers of Ukraine – the allowed deduction by the corporate taxpayer is limited to 85% of the incurred expenses;
- Expenses, which are not related to the business activities of the corporate taxpayer, are not deductible; and
- Certain types of payments to affiliated persons are not deductible.

Taxation of Non-Residents

The CIT Law establishes the following general principles with respect to the taxation of foreign legal entities:

- Foreign legal entities will be taxed in Ukraine on their profits derived from their commercial activities undertaken on the territory of Ukraine through a permanent establishment; and
- Income derived from sources within the territory of Ukraine by non-residents, which are not engaged in commercial activities on the territory of Ukraine through a permanent establishment, will be taxed at the time of the remittance of such income to such non-residents, and such taxes will be withheld from the sums remitted.

The CIT Law provides that a non-resident will be liable to pay CIT with respect to all Ukrainian-source income. "Ukrainian-source income" is defined as any income derived by non-residents from any business activities on the territory of Ukraine. Article 13.1 enumerates the various categories of income, which are per se deemed to be Ukrainian-source income, including, inter alia: interest payments, dividends, royalties, lease payments, proceeds from real estate sales on the territory of Ukraine, profits from securities transactions, profits from Joint Activity Agreements or long-term agreements, broker or agency fees, and other kinds of income derived by a non-resident (or the permanent establishment of such non-resident, or any other non-resident) from its business activity on the territory of Ukraine.

However, the CIT Law provides that the income of non-residents received in the form of a payment or other kind of compensation for the value of goods (works or services) transferred (or delivered) by a non-resident (or its permanent establishment) to a resident shall not constitute Ukrainian-source income.

The CIT Law provides for a 15% withholding tax rate (defined as the "repatriation tax") to be withheld by a resident taxpayer or by a permanent establishment of such non-resident from the amount of any Ukrainian-source income if and when such non-resident's Ukrainian-source income is remitted to such non-resident by a resident taxpayer or by a permanent establishment of such non-resident, unless and applicable bilateral double taxation treaty provides relief with respect of such repatriation tax.

Dividends received by a non-resident legal entity from its ownership rights in a resident legal entity are taxed at a 15% withholding tax rate, unless an applicable bilateral double taxation treaty provides otherwise.

Ukraine is a party to more than 40 bilateral double taxation treaties that provide special rules for determination of permanent establishment, Ukrainian-source income, withholding tax rates, etc.

Taxation of Permanent Establishments

As mentioned above, for purposes of the CIT Law, permanent establishments of non-residents are deemed to be independent taxpayers in Ukraine. Under Article 1.17 of the CIT Law, a permanent establishment of a non-resident in Ukraine is created through a fixed place of business, through which the business activities of such non-resident are either fully or partially conducted in Ukraine. The concept of a "permanent establishment" under the CIT Law is similar to the definition adopted in the majority of the bilateral double taxation treaties, to which Ukraine is a party, although the definition under the CIT Law is somewhat broader.

The CIT Law provides that income derived by a non-resident, which conducts its business activities in Ukraine through a permanent establishment, is subject to taxation at the general tax rate, which is currently 30%.

Value-Added Tax

The Law of Ukraine on the "Value-Added Tax", as amended (the VAT Law), is the principal law governing VAT in Ukraine. In accordance with Article 2 of the VAT Law, any Ukrainian or non-Ukrainian legal entity will be required to pay VAT, if, inter alia, that person:

- Has sold goods (or provided works, services) subject to VAT during any period within the last 12 calendar months, with an aggregate value in excess of 3,600 times of non-taxable personal minimal income; or
- Imports (ships) goods into the customs territory of Ukraine; or

- Is the recipient of works (services) from a non-resident entity and such works (services) are provided for consumption within the customs territory of Ukraine.

The VAT Law identifies a list of transactions subject to VAT, which includes, inter alia, the following transactions:

- The sale of goods (or the provision of works, services) on and within the customs territory of Ukraine;
- The import of goods into the customs territory of Ukraine;
- The import of works (services) from non-residents in circumstances, in which such works (services) are provided for consumption within the customs territory of Ukraine.

Transactions, which do not constitute taxable events, subject to VAT include, inter alia:

- The issuance, placement, and cash sale of securities;
- Lease payments pursuant to a financial lease agreement or a residential lease agreement (provided that it is the lessee's principal residence);
- The transfer of pledged property pursuant to a loan agreement and its return to the pledgor after the expiry of such agreement;
- The providing of insurance and reinsurance services; and
- The contribution of fixed assets to the charter fund of a legal entity in exchange for ownership rights in such legal entity.

The VAT Law provides for a tax rate of 20% of the contractual value of the relevant goods (works, services), which value includes any excise tax, import duty, and other taxes or payments required by applicable Ukrainian legislation. A zero percent tax rate is provided by the VAT Law for goods (works, services) exported (provided, rendered) outside of the customs territory of Ukraine.

CIT, VAT, Land Tax and Customs Privileges for Technology Innovation Projects

The Innovation Law provides for the following CIT, VAT and customs privileges for technology innovation activity.

Provided that the implementation of a registered innovation project has started within eighteen months from the date of registration and for the term of registration (3 years), a tax payer who qualifies as a subject of innovation activity receives a 50% relief on VAT on the sale of goods (Services) produced/rendered within the scope of its innovation project and 50% relief on CIT on profits generated by such taxpayer from its activities related to the innovation project. The saved funds are accumulated on a special account and may be used by the taxpayer exclusively for further financing of the innovation activity. The taxpayer who is granted the above privileges is required to carry out separate accounting for its innovation project.

If more than 70% of the aggregate value of an enterprise's goods/services is produced/rendered within the scope of an innovation project, such enterprise has the right to the accelerated depreciation of some of its capital assets at the annual rate of 20%. In addition, such enterprise pays the land tax at 50% of the usual rate.

Under the innovation Law, imported raw materials, equipment, spare parts and other goods, apart from excisable ones, that are necessary for a priority innovation project but are not produced in Ukraine or, although produced locally, are not of appropriate quality, are exempt from import duties and import VAT. Importers who avail themselves of the above privilege are required to submit quarterly reports to the customs authorities on the use of the imported goods.

CIT, VAT, Customs and Currency Privileges for Technoparks

Under the Technopark Law technoparks (which, for these purposes, include their subsidiaries and/or joint ventures) enjoy special CIT and VAT tax breaks in the amount of 100% of CIT and VAT from the income generated from the implementation of their respective technology innovation projects. The above sums of CIT and VAT are also accumulated on a special bank account and are to be used only for purposes of further reinvesting into their technology innovating projects.

Technoparks are also relieved from paying customs duties and import VAT goods, apart from excisable ones, which are necessary for purposes of implementing their respective technology innovation projects, but are not produced in Ukraine or, although produced locally, are not of appropriate quality.

Technoparks are also provided with the privilege of having their foreign currency proceeds repatriated into Ukraine within 150 calendar days as opposed to 90 calendar days under the general currency control regime applicable to all other Ukrainian taxpayers

20

Zambian Report on the New IPR Regime under the TRIPS for Developing Countries

Joseph Simbaya

(National Institute for Scientific and Industrial Research, Livestock and Pest Research Centre, Private Bag 350049, Chilanga, Zambia)

INTRODUCTION

In Zambia, all the GATT agreement incorporating Trade Related aspects of Intellectual Property Rights (TRIPS) are administered through the Patents and Companies Registration Office (PCRO) which is an executive agency of the Ministry of Commerce, Trade and Industry (MCTI). The PCRO is currently undergoing both commercialization and computerisation to meet trends in the national economy and Government policy on public service reform. In keeping with its *role* in the economy, its' mission is To promote innovation, orderly trade and the competitiveness of Zambian industry and commerce through the provision *of* information and the registration system of commercial and intellectual property rights.

FUNCTION

The mission reflects the organisation's three basic functions. The first being to run a legal system *for* registration and protection *of* commercial property (*i.e.*, companies and firms and attendant particulars like bank mortgages) and industrial property (*i.e.*, trade marks, designs and patents for inventions). Since the PCRO is empowered to sell these services, collection of revenue for the Central Treasury is the organisation's second function. The third function rests in the Office's position as the legal depository of the information tendered for registration. This is rich commercial and technological information which the organisation access to investors and other entrepreneurs.

CURRENT LEGISLATION

The industrial property legislation of Zambia comprises the following: the Patents Act, 1957 (Chapter 692), which provides for a nationally independent system of patent protection with no fields of technology excluded and a patent term of sixteen years (with a possibility of extension); the Registered Designs Act, 1958 (Chapter 696), which provides for a registration system without an opposition procedure and a term of protection of five years renewable for two consecutive periods of five years each; and the Trade Marks Act, 1958 (Chapter 693), which provides for a registration system, publication of applications, an opposition procedure, and a term of protection or seven years renewable for periods of fourteen years and the Merchandise Marks Act, 1958 (Chapter 694) relating to the marking of goods and matters incidental thereto.

PROVISIONS INCONSISTENT WITH TRIPS OBLIGATIONS

Trade (and Service Marks)

The Trade Marks Act, which provides protection only for goods will require amendments to provide protection for trademarks also for services (TRI PS Part II Section 2);

Section 9 (rights conferred) of the Trade Marks Act will require to be expanded to provide protection against use of identical or similar signs for goods or services that are identical or similar (TRIPS Article 16.1):

Specific provisions will require to be inserted in the Trade Marks Act on well-known marks in compliance with TRIPS Article 16.2 and 16.3 (The Act, in its Section 32 only provides for the defensive registration, for other goods, of marks which have become well-known in respect of the goods for which they have been registered and used,);

Section 31 (I)(a) (removal from register on grounds of non-use) of the Trade Marks Act will require to be amended, in compliance with TRI PS article 19.1, to provide that a mark may be removed only after an uninterrupted period of at least three years of non-use (Section 31(1) (b) contains a similar provision in which the period of non-use specified is five years or more and therefore complies with TRIPS Article 19.1).

Patents

Section 28(4) (rights conferred) of the Patents Act will require to be amended to conform to TRI PS Article 28. 1;

Section 29(a) (term of patent) of the Patents Act will require to he modified in order to comply with TRIPS Article 33;

Section 37 (compulsory licenses in case of abuse or insufficient use of patent rights) will require to he redrafted in the light of the requirement in TRIPS Article 27. 1 that patent rights shall be enjoyable irrespective of whether products arc imported or locally produced and in the light of obligations under TRIPS Article 31. In particular, the provisions of subsection (6)(a) (non-working), subsection (6)(b) (working being prevented or hindered by importation), subsection (8) (the possibility of compulsory licenses being exclusive) and subsection (11) (divesting the patent owner of tile right to use tile invention) will be affected;

Section 38 (issuance of non-voluntary licenses in respect of inventions relating to food, medicine or curative devices) will require deletion in the light of the requirement in TRIPS Article 27.1 that patent rights shall be enjoyable without discrimination as to the field of technology. The statement, above on compulsory licenses and the requirements of TRIPS Article 31 would equally apply;

Section 40 (use of patented inventions for services of the State) will require to be redrafted in the light of obligations under TRIPS Article 31;

Section 50 (revocation of patents) will require to be modified in its subsection (2) which, by a cross-reference to Section 37(6), provides that non working or working being impaired by importation are grounds for revocation (please see statement, above, on Section 31 and the requirements of TRIPS Article 27.1);

Section 53 (procedure and conditions in action for infringement) will require to be modified in order 10 ensure that its subsection (6) fully incorporates the requirements of TRIPS Article 34 with regard to the reversal of the burden of proof in cases of infringement of a patent which is a process for obtaining a product;

Layout-Designs (Topographies) of Integrated Circuits (TRIPS Part II Section 6).

SUBJECT MATTER FOR WHICH PROTECTION, REQUIRED UNDER TRIPS IS NOT PROVIDED UNDER THE CURRENT LEGISLATION

Geographical Indications (TRIPS Part II Section 3)

It is noted that the Trade Marks Act, in its Parts IX (certification trademarks) provides for the registration of certification marks, which are defined, in Section 42(1) as marks adapted, in relation to any goods, to distinguish, in the course of trade, goods certified by any person in respect of origin, material, mode or manufacture quality, accuracy or other characteristic, from goods not so certified. Thus some degree of protection could be available for geographical indications through their registration as certification trademarks. Further, under the Merchandise Marks Act, it is an offense to apply to goods a false trade description (including any description, statement or other indication. direct or indirect, as to the place or country in which any goods were manufactured, made, produced. assembled or mixed). The above mentioned provisions, however, do not meet the obligations in TRIPS Part II Section 3 in respect of geographical indications as therein defined.

Special Requirements Related to Border Measures (TRIPS Part III (Enforcement) Section 4)

To the extent that the procedures set out in TRIPS Part III Section 4 are not available under the general civil law or under laws relating to Customs authorities (see Part IV, below, on enforcement and other acts prohibited) the Merchandise Marks Act state that it is an offence to forget a trademark or to falsely apply to goods any trademark or any mark so nearly resembling it as to be likely to deceive.

Intellectual Property Rights

The problem of intellectual property rights in many of the developing countries is of major concern in as far as implementing TRIPS agreement requirements, this is because most developing countries ownership of resources such as land, water, plants seeds including indigenous knowledge is community based. In rural areas, all resources in a community belong to the community and are for the benefit of the whole community and no individual can have a claim on anything. The belief is that any special knowledge or technique is a gift from God and should be used to the benefit *of* the community through sharing to the community, these values need to recognized and maintained under the TRIPS agreement. They should not be affected by market globalization.

TRIPS and Farmers Rights

Most of the developing nations especially in Africa are still struggling to feed their populations. Current laws on TRIPS with regard to plant breeding and Biotechnology may adversely affect agricultural development more especially in rural areas. TRIPS should, therefore, allow communities, individuals farmers and Government agencies to have access to new innovations to enable them meet food security and promote bio-diversity. It must be noted that most of the Scientists in the developing world are employed by Government agencies and depend on tax payers for their salaries. Thus, these people must benefit from any innovations coming from the scientific community with minimal restrictions. Further more, in most cases scientists exploit community resources in their innovations without paying for royalties or asking for permission from the same community. It is therefore important that the community should benefit from innovations developed in the areas by local scientists.

The IPR regime and the TRIPS agreement must recognize community rights, indigenous knowledge and farmers rights as a distinct frame work that is essential to developing countries which should not meet patent law requirement under TRIPS.

TRIPS should endeavour to protect and enhance the development of indigenous peoples Knowledge in their effort to promote Bio-diversity and food security. This may be done by ensuring that rural communities have full access to information and the use of available innovations in their communities.

TRIPS should also encourage developing countries to maintain their systems for innovation and Knowledge creation which is essential in their quest for development.

In order to address the above concerns under the TRIPS agreement on IPR, the country through the PCRO is in the process of establishing a National Committee on Intellectual Properly Rights. The committee will consist of representatives from various interest groups and stakeholders including the Ministry of Commerce and Trade, Zambia Chamber of Commerce, Universities and Research Institutions. The Functions of the committee will be to:

1. Assess TRIPS agreements implications on the Zambian national economy
2. Formulate appropriate legislations which will enable Zambian laws to be adapted to the TRIPS agreement.
3. Assess implications of special articles such as 27.3 (b) in as they affect National Development interests,
4. Attend to any other issues that may arise from the committees functions.

The committee will also give a report to consider legislations and policy making issues. Other areas that need to addressed by the Zambian Government for it to comply with TRIPS include the Undisclosed Information (TRIPS Part II Section 7) and the Plant Varieties (TRIPS Article 27.3(b)). The latter is somehow being enforced through the Ministry of Agriculture, Food and Fisheries through the Research Branch and the Seed Control and Certification Institute (SCCI). There is need for these institutions to collaborate with the PCRO.

Enforcement

The legal system of Zambia is the Common Law system which has absorbed certain principles of Roman-Dutch Law. Matters relating to evidence, injunctions (interdicts), damages and other remedies arc dealt with under the general law of civil procedure for all civil wrongs. However, the following express provisions are noteworthy: in respect of infringement proceedings. Section 53(5) of the Patents Act refers to court orders for an injunction, interdict, damages, inspection or account: and Sections 7 and 10(2) of the Trade Marks Act refer to proceedings to prevent and to recover damages for infringement and the remedies of injunction, interdict and other reliefs.

Although the Trade Marks Act docs not provide for criminal procedures and penalties for willful trademark counterfeiting (TRIPS Article 61). Section 3 (application of trademarks and trade descriptions), Section 4 (certain acts deemed to be forgery of a trademark) and Section 5 (forgery of a trademark).

ACKNOWLEDGEMENTS

Very special thanks are due to Mr. Wilbroad Mulenga, Assistant Registrar at the Zambia Patent Office for the provision of materials used in this report. Mrs. Tamara Kambikambi of the Crop Science Department at the University of Zambia is also acknowledged for materials on Intellectual Property Rights and farmers rights.

21

The Current Status of Intellectual Porperty Laws and How They Relate to TRIPS and Other International Undertakings

J.M. Gopo

[Director, Biotechnology Research Institute (Bri), SIRDC, P O Box 6640, Harae, Zimbabwe]

INTRODUCTION

Intellectual Property Laws of Zimbabwe are governed by five (5) main pieces of legislation namely the Patents Act of Zimbabwe (Chapter 26-03). Trade Marks Act Chapter 25-04) the Industrial Designs Act of Zimbabwe (Chapter 26:02) the Plant Breeders Act of Zimbabwe and the Copyright Act (Chapter 26:01). In this paper I will concentrate on the Patents Act of Zimbabwe and examine its relationship to TRIPS and its Convention on Biological Diversity (CBD). The last part of the paper explores possible solutions to the harmonisation of the various pieces of legislation so as to provide effective and productive protection regimes for Zimbabwe

THE PATENTS ACTS OF ZIMBABWE

The Act provides protection to any new and useful art (whether producing a physical effect or not), process, machine, manufacture or composition of matter which is not obvious or any new and useful improvement thereof which is not obvious, capable of being used and applied in trade or industry. The term of protection is twenty years (20) through renewals after which a Patent falls domain to public use. The requirements for patentability are:

- The Invention must be novel/or new
- Must involve an "inventive step" *i.e.* technically non-obvious
- Must be applicable through an industrial process.

The Patent Act of Zimbabwe does not cover the following:

- Discovery of a hitherto unknown substance which exist in nature.
- Scientific theories and mathematical methods
- Computer programs and methods of presenting information and others that do not qualify in the mentioned requirement of patentability are excluded from patenting.

If the three requirements are met, then, whether it is a product or a process, in any field, it is granted Patent Protection. This therefore, means that in Agricultural Biotechnology can also be granted patent protection if the aforementioned requirements of patentability are met. Failure to meet these requirements, then another form of protection in the form of Plant Breeders Rights are available. According to our Plant Breeders Rights Act, varieties are eligible for protection if they are distinct from existing and commonly known varieties sufficiently homogenous, stable and new (in commercialisation sense) This means that the breeders Protection extends only to the production of reproductive material for purposes of commercial marketing (as distinct from the use of the protected variety as an initial source of creating varieties) and to the use of the registered name for selling any other variety within the *same* class. *

*UK Green Paper "Intellectual Property Rights and Innovations" page 35 (1983).

REFUSAL OF APPLICATIONS IN CERTAIN CASES

The Registrar of Patents may refuse according to our Act, any application for a patent that.

- Is frivolous on the ground that it claims as invention anything obviously contrary to well-established natural laws or
- The use of the invention in respect of which the application is made would be contrary to law or
- It claims as an invention a substance capable of being used as food or medicine which is a mixture of known ingredients possessing only the aggregate of the known properties of the ingredients or that it claims as an invention a process producing such a substance by mere add mixture.

UK Green Paper: "Intellectual Property Rights and Innovations" page 35 (1983). It is appears to the Registrar that any invention in respect of which an application for a patent is made might be used contrary to law, he or she may refuse the application unless the specification is amended by the insertion of such disclaimer in respect of that use of the invention or such other reference to the illegality thereof.

It must however, be mentioned that our Act also provides for an appeal system where aggrieved parties will appeal to the Patents Tribunal, which is chaired by a President (who is a Judge of the High Court).

REGIONAL AND INTERNATIONAL TREATIES

Zimbabwe is party to ARIPO (African Regional Industrial Property Organisation) under the Lusaka Agreement of 1976. She is a signatory to both the Harare Protocol (for protection of Patents and Industrial Designs) and the Banjul Protocol (for the Protection of Trade Marks). We are also party to the Patent Co-operation Treaty and a member of WIPO (World Intellectual Property Organisation). Last but not least, Zimbabwe is party to the World trade Organisation and also party to TRIPS. She has been given up to the year 2000 to comply with the Provisions of TRIPS and the Department of Intellectual Property is actively working with relevant Ministries and Stakeholders to ensure Zimbabwe's compliance by the given deadline.

A number of institutions and organizations in Zimbabwe are not satisfied with the status of IPR-Patents in Zimbabwe. The current Patent laws do not offer protection to a number of organised groups such as the Zimbabwe National Traditional Healers Association- (ZINATHA). The current patent law does not offer protection on indigenous knowledge - systems and traditional knowledge systems of Zimbabwe. Debate showed that there was need to develop a *Sui-generis Legislation on IPR-Patents for Zimbabwe.*

The Biotechnology Research Institute (BRI) of the Scientific and Industrial Research and Development Centre (SIRDC) in collaboration with Community Technology Trust (CTDT) held a National Workshop aimed at developing a *sui-generis* legislation for Zimbabwe. The workshop showed that Zimbabwe needs to review the Implications of signed and ratified international conventions such as the GTT/TRIPS agreements and the Convention on Biological Diversity (CBD). The country needs to develop a *sui-generis legislation which is* in conformity with *GATT/WTO* and the CBD articles. To facilitate this process there is need to consult the relevant stakeholders, define what is parentable define the regimes of protection required and identify the interface between and among the various players, in Zimbabwe. It was shown that if Zimbabwe is to develop an effective *sui-generis* legislation a number of issues need to be assessed and reviewed and threes include:

- A review of similar legislations from both developed and developing countries:
- Defining the protectable subject matter of the *sui-generis* system, taking into account the interests of the different stakeholders and their socio-economic and cultural practices;
- Defining protection regimes required to protect traditional knowledges, innovations and technologies of both the formal and informal sectors including interface between the two systems:
- Defining the scope of protection within such a *sui-generis* system so that it provides attributes, privileges and benefits to the owner or holder of such

innovation. technology or traditional knowledge, which is allowed under the TRIPS Agreement.

- The aspects of Traditional Resource Rights (TRR) should be viewed within the context of different types of rights relating to the traditional or customary use of resources through local (farming) communities. Traditional resource right are widely recognized by different instruments such as, the CBD, the FAO Undertaking and the ILO Convention 169. This aspect needs to be addressed in the Zimbabwean context and legislative provisions provided.

WORKSHOP OBJECTIVES

The overall objective of the workshop was to develop a model *sui-generis* IPR-Patent Legislation for Zimbabwe, which is compatible with international conventions signed and ratified by government.

OUTPUTS

Zimbabwe has successfully carried out a:

- Review on processes and forms of legislation from other developed and developing countries which have established *sui-generis* legislation.
- Has discussed the three commissioned thematic papers and develop draft documents on such issues as: forms of protection, patentable subject matter, national sovereignty and access to genetic resources, technology transform benefit sharing and traditional knowledges and resource rights. The draft legislation proposals has been harmonized with international conventions and
- Agreement signed and ratified by government taking into account the socio-economic and cultural realities of Zimbabwe.
- Has drafted and formulated a model legislation for Zimbabwe and has been submitted to the Research Council of Zimbabwe for onward submission to the Attorney General's Office for consideration as a white paper legislative purposes.
- Zimbabwe has used the draft white paper for regional (SADC) consultative at a Regional Workshop on IPR-Patent.